"Bipolar disorder represents one of _____ ing mental health conditions. Self-mar _____ e a critical part of achieving optimal he _____ when living with the condition. *Preventing Bipolar Relapse* represents a valuable resource for people who are newly diagnosed, struggling, or just wanting to learn from someone who has been there how best to stay in balance. Packed full of evidence-informed tips and tools, this accessible and pragmatic book offers ways for people with bipolar disorder to flourish."

—**Erin Michalak,** associate professor in the department of psychiatry at the University of British Columbia in Vancouver, Canada, and coeditor of *Practical Management of Bipolar Disorder*

"*Preventing Bipolar Relapse* is an essential guide for the consumer and caregiver alike. White's SNAP approach gives the reader an easy method to successfully navigate the complexities of bipolar disorder. Her personal experience offers hope, encouragement, and the tools to prevent relapse."

—**Muffy Walker, MSN, MBA,** founder and chairman of the board at the International Bipolar Foundation

"Maintaining stabilization and relapse prevention is one of the most important and challenging aspects of treatment for bipolar disorder. This is a topic that has rarely been addressed in the integrative way White spells out in her book. Highly recommended…both for those suffering from bipolar disorder and their loved ones."

—**John Preston, PsyD,** professor emeritus with Alliant International University, Sacramento

WITHDRAWN

Preventing Bipolar Relapse

a lifestyle program to help you maintain a balanced mood & live well

RUTH C. WHITE
PhD, MPH, MSW

New Harbinger Publications, Inc.

Publisher's Note

This publication is designed to provide accurate and authoritative information in regard to the subject matter covered. It is sold with the understanding that the publisher is not engaged in rendering psychological, financial, legal, or other professional services. If expert assistance or counseling is needed, the services of a competent professional should be sought.

"Weekly Medication Log" adapted from "Chart 3.1: Medication Log"; "Weekly Triggers and Mood Chart" adapted from "Chart 4.2: Tracking Moods and Triggers"; "Daily Mood and Food Tracker" adapted from "Action Step 8.1: Log Your Daily Food Intake"; "Weekly Meal Plan" adapted from "Action Step 8.3: Create Your Meal Plan"; all in BIPOLAR 101 © 2009 Ruth C. White and John Preston. Used by permission of New Harbinger Publications, Inc.

Distributed in Canada by Raincoast Books

Copyright © 2014 by Ruth C. White
            New Harbinger Publications, Inc.
            5674 Shattuck Avenue
            Oakland, CA 94609
            www.newharbinger.com

Cover design by Amy Shoup; Acquired by Melissa Kirk; Edited by Will DeRooy

All Rights Reserved

Library of Congress Cataloging-in-Publication Data on file

Printed in the United States of America

16   15   14

10 9 8 7 6 5 4 3 2 1   First printing

CONTENTS

ACKNOWLEDGMENTS

I would like to thank my incredibly talented medical team at Group Health Cooperative in Seattle, including my psychiatrist, Dr. Donna Lohmann, and my psychotherapist, Mike Welsch, MSW, for helping me learn how to prevent relapse of my bipolar symptoms and for always being there when I needed them—in person, by phone, or by e-mail. They taught me how to trust my knowledge of my illness and my knowledge of myself so that I could take the steps I needed to maintain my health while living the full life I want to live and having the productive career I want to have. Of course there were times when my symptoms (or unhealthy habits) got the best of me and broke my years of quiet; but that is the nature of the beast that is bipolar disorder.

Thank you to all the folks in the various Facebook groups that provide support for people affected by bipolar disorder, many of whom agreed to share with me (and you) their ways of preventing bipolar relapse, some of which I have included in this book.

Thanks to acquisitions editor Melissa Kirk for her patience, support, and guidance; for proposing the idea for this book; and for suggesting that I write it. And to Will DeRooy, my copyeditor, who made sure the words were where they should be.

A huge thank-you to my research assistant, Matthew Pritchard, a student at Seattle University, without whose long hours on research databases and meticulous preparation of my references this manuscript would not have been completed on time. His hard work, discipline, timeliness, and high standards have set the bar high for research assistants to come. I expect great things of him.

I want to thank my parents for always telling me I could do whatever I wanted and supporting me as I attempted to do just that. I am forever grateful to the friends and family who supported me when my symptoms would return. Your patience and love got me through. Last, I want to thank my daughter, Maya, who always makes me laugh and inspires me with her confidence in herself and the possibilities of life. She is also my inspiration for doing everything I can to prevent my own bipolar relapse.

INTRODUCTION

Finding out that you have bipolar disorder can be unsettling and scary. It may be difficult to accept that you have a chronic illness that requires medication and lifelong management. Yet acceptance is the first step to getting and staying better. Once you accept that you have bipolar disorder, with the right combination of lifestyle changes, medication, and therapy, you can manage it successfully. That is the focus of this book.

The steps to managing your bipolar disorder and preventing relapse may be simple, but they are not always easy. Preventing bipolar relapse requires motivation, a commitment to your own health, discipline, structure, courage, and a belief that you can get better. You need effective and creative strategies for promoting your own healthy behavior and for avoiding the recurrence of your bipolar symptoms. Success at preventing bipolar relapse also requires the help of others such as your friends, your partner, your family, and your health care providers. If you have bipolar disorder and want to live a healthier, more balanced life, this book is for you. This is a book that I hope will help you manage your illness by reducing the frequency and severity of your symptoms so that you can improve the quality of your life.

MY STORY

In 2004, I was diagnosed with bipolar disorder. (I personally prefer the term "manic depression," because it more accurately reflects the two conditions that are described by the more modern "bipolar disorder.") By that time, I had already had symptoms of the disorder for twenty years, and I had learned how to manage some of the more obvious ones. For example, I learned early in my life that exercise made me feel really good and kept my mood stable and my brain clear. Later, I also realized that caffeinated drinks made me wired and sometimes irritable. So I would try to get in a walk or swim three to five times a week and keep my caffeine intake limited to one medium cup of a caffeinated beverage before noon. Since my teenage years I had kept a journal, so I had begun to also understand the influence of my menstrual cycle on the way I was feeling. My journal helped confirm my bipolar diagnosis because it clearly showed that I had experienced manic and depressive episodes (although I had not recognized them as such). It allowed my mental health care provider to see patterns over time and helped me understand how my illness presented in my particular case, affecting my behavior and my life.

I am a social work professor, and I have been employed as a social worker in various mental health settings for many years. That does not mean that I always do everything I know I should to stay healthy. Some days I do not feel like I care about staying healthy, and other days I feel like I do not have the energy. But for the most part, I know that I do not like being manic (unlike some people with bipolar disorder) or depressed; nor do I like to experience any of the symptoms of my illness. (Though the experience of hypomania is quite enjoyable for me, I am always afraid that it may lead to mania, so the fear that it creates limits my enjoyment of its more obvious benefits, such as creativity and productivity). This book grew out of my own struggle to stay healthy while still "having a life," which included a career that I had fought hard to build (and which hypomania had kept going). I wanted to be a stable parent for my daughter. I wanted to be able to reduce my medication intake, because of its undesirable side effects and also its impact on my bank balance. I also do not want to spend another week in a psychiatric hospital, as I did in the fall of 2007. After being released from hospital, I spent a lot of time researching bipolar disorder so that I could better understand my illness and what was required if I was to be, and stay, healthy. I cowrote *Bipolar 101* (published in 2009) to help people who have just been diagnosed with bipolar disorder understand the disorder and its treatment. To this day, I maintain a blog about bipolar disorder at http://bipolar-101.blogspot.com. In it, I explore some of the issues relevant to having bipolar disorder, with a focus on the latest research, distilled for a nonscientific audience.

Just because I write about bipolar disorder does not mean that I have bipolar disorder all figured out or that I follow all the strategies I present all the time. Like other people with chronic illnesses, I do not always want to live with illness at the center of my life. I want to have that drink of alcohol (or that third drink). I really want that jolt of caffeine in the afternoon, even though it will affect my ability to sleep. I want to stay out late into the night and not worry about how sleep deprivation will affect my mood in the morning or for days or weeks after. I get lazy and do not want to exercise even though I know how much better I will feel, how less likely I will be to have a mood episode, or how much better the quality of my sleep will be. So I wrote this book as much for me as for other people living with bipolar disorder.

THE STIGMA OF MENTAL ILLNESS

I wrote this book knowing the stigma faced by people living with mental illness such as bipolar disorder. This stigma often prevents people with mental illness from making positive changes in their life, because they do not want to "out" themselves to friends, relatives, or work colleagues and superiors as having a mental illness. As a speaker against stigma, I know that even the most educated audiences have negative stereotypes about people like you and me, partly because people who work in mental health tend to see us when we are ill and not when we are healthy.

Healthy living with bipolar disorder is like healthy living with diabetes. When you make an effort to stay healthy, nobody notices that you have the disorder, and you blend in with the people around you. You do not "win" all the time, but you get on with your life while dealing with your disorder, knowing that it is just a fact of life and a part of your experience. You do not ignore your disorder, but neither do you let it run your life. Those of us who live with bipolar disorder know that we are more than the nature of our brains. Staying healthy helps us be in more control of our lives, maximize our productivity, and participate in rewarding daily activities.

DIAGNOSIS AND RECOVERY

If you have been diagnosed with bipolar disorder, it was probably due to a major mood episode in which your functioning was impaired. Your path to health most likely involves talk therapy with psychotherapists, as well as psychiatric visits to find the right combination of medications that will keep future mood episodes at bay. In the meantime, you may struggle with the fear that your bipolar symptoms may return without warning and the fact that you may have no control over whether or when this may happen. That fear is real, because there is no cure for bipolar disorder and sometimes it is hard to predict when a mood episode will come, how long it will last, and how severe it will be.

Therefore, trying to prevent mood episodes is a goal for most people living with bipolar disorder. This book will address some useful strategies for maximizing your mental well-being so that even if you do have mood episodes, they will be less intense and not last as long. However, the ultimate goal is to have no more mood episodes at all. This book gives you the best chance of this, using the best strategies based on the latest scientific evidence.

SNAP: SLEEP, NUTRITION, ACTIVITY, PEOPLE

The focus of this book is SNAP—a four-part approach to managing bipolar symptoms that, in conjunction with monitoring your symptoms and tracking your triggers, can go a long way toward reducing the frequency and severity of those symptoms. SNAP stands for Sleep, Nutrition, Activity, and People. It is based on scientific evidence that healthy sleep patterns, good nutrition, regular physical activity, and having a social support network, in addition to taking effective medications as prescribed and participating in psychotherapy as needed, are important to managing bipolar disorder.

There is no "magic bullet" that will make your bipolar symptoms disappear for good, but the more strategies you employ to help your brain function at its best, the more successful you will be at preventing bipolar relapse. At first it may seem like a lot of work, but it is likely that you are already doing some things right, and once you find out what works best for you, you can make it part of a lifestyle that supports your mental well-being and prevents bipolar relapse. Let's look briefly at each of the parts of the SNAP approach.

- **Sleep** management is important to all people at all stages of life, but it is particularly important for people with mental illness like bipolar disorder. Sleep regulates your circadian rhythm, which research is increasingly finding to be important to mood regulation in people living with bipolar disorder. Getting good sleep that allows you to wake up feeling rested and energized is not only evidence that you are probably not experiencing symptoms of your bipolar disorder; it can also prevent you having a relapse.

- **Nutrition** provides the building blocks for body functioning, and a healthy body helps support a healthy mind. A basic nutrition plan for someone with bipolar disorder involves eating generally recommended foods, with a focus on foods that help the brain function and prevent episodes of depression and mania. Micronutrients like omega-3 fatty acids help with the balance of biochemicals such as serotonin and epinephrine, which influence mood episodes.

- **Activity** has a broad meaning in our discussion. Although it is focused on physical activity and includes formal exercise (exercise for its own sake), it also may refer to living an active lifestyle that may not require formal exercise. We will talk about how activity influences your brain and body functions to maximize your brain health, and I will provide you with strategies that will help support the physical and mental health you desire.

- **People** focuses on the ways in which the people in your life can help you maintain an even keel and support you in your healthy behaviors. It is also true that interacting with people helps decrease the likelihood of depression and decreases the severity and duration of depressive symptoms. There will also be a discussion of medical and mental health professionals for dispensing of medications and/or for talk therapy.

MEDICATION

The standard treatment of bipolar disorder includes a wide variety of medications. Some of these medications are mood stabilizers, some are antidepressants, and some are antianxiety medications that reduce the impact of stress and are also sometimes used to promote restful sleep. Because of the complexity of the illness, because no two people have exactly the same symptoms, because no two people will have exactly the same reaction to a particular medication, and because of possible side effects and drug interactions, finding and consistently taking the right medication often is the most challenging aspect of a course of treatment for bipolar disorder.

Sometimes it takes a lot of trial and error, and therefore a lot of patience, to find the right combination of medications that work for you. Once you find that combination, it is important to stick with the regimen as prescribed so that your medications can work as they should. In fact, the first chapter in this book discusses the importance of taking medications as prescribed and offers strategies for following medication regimens to prevent you from experiencing bipolar relapse.

TRACKING AND MONITORING YOUR TRIGGERS AND MOOD

In this book we will explore the importance of each aspect of SNAP (sleep, nutrition, activity, and people) using the latest information from medical science. I will outline methods for integrating certain relapse prevention strategies into your life and give you tools (or point you to resources) to support your efforts to manage your behaviors, monitor for triggers, and track your progress in preventing bipolar relapse. You can also download these tools from the publisher's website for this book: http://www.newharbinger.com/28814.

The importance of tracking the elements of your mental well-being cannot be overemphasized. These elements include good mental health hygiene, such as good sleep, regular exercise, and the presence of social support networks, and the absence of any symptoms of bipolar disorder, such as depression, mania, and anxiety. Tracking allows you to monitor yourself so that you can know when you are at risk for relapse and can intervene before you have a full-blown mood episode. For example, if you realize that you have not been getting a good night's sleep, you may expect to have some depression in the coming days, depending on how long your poor sleep lasts, or it may signal to you that you may be experiencing hypomanic or manic symptoms. You can then use some of the strategies in the book to divert or minimize a mood episode.

By keeping track of your triggers and mood, you can take action before symptoms of your bipolar disorder arise or before they increase in severity. Monitoring also will help you know when you may need outside help. Furthermore, tracking your own well-being will also help your health care providers assist you to the best of their ability. Many times it is easy to forget when your symptoms began, what preceded them, or how their severity compares to other incidences of illness in your life. Having monitoring and tracking tools provides useful information for maintaining your mental well-being.

If you follow the recommendations in this book and make them a lifestyle, you will find that your mood is more stable and you can more effectively deal with daily challenges without precipitating a mood episode. What I mean by making these recommendations a lifestyle is following them simply as a way of life and not necessarily as a treatment for an illness. View them as basic health strategies that have been tailored for people living with bipolar disorder, and make them a habit.

I am not saying that this will be easy; it can be hard to change old habits and form new ones, even when doing so is in the interest of your long-term mental health. It may help you to know that sleep, nutrition, activity, and people are connected; for example, exercise can help you get better sleep. In other words, the interrelatedness between these areas of your life means that making changes in one area results in changes in others. For that reason, do not worry too much about the strategies that you have difficulty with. Focus on what you can do that is helpful, and you will find that you do less of the things that are unhelpful.

ACHIEVING YOUR GOAL OF BIPOLAR RELAPSE PREVENTION

The overall goal is for you to get healthy and stay healthy, and the steps outlined in this book will help you do that. At various points in this book, you will be encouraged to set smaller goals for yourself in areas such as sleep and exercise, and the book will help you develop strategies for reaching those goals. Writing down goals helps you reach them by making them concrete and reminding you of where you want to go and what you want to do. The book also provides you with tools to track your progress. These tools are found in the chapters on sleep, nutrition, and activity and also in the chapter on tracking, which provides a comprehensive tracking tool. There are also tracking tools that are available for download from the website related to this book.

This book is just one piece of a comprehensive plan to help you manage a challenging and often debilitating chronic mental illness. The plan includes good sleep, physical activity, good nutrition, and good interpersonal relations. It also includes taking your medications as prescribed and building an ongoing relationship with a mental health care provider. Because research on bipolar disorder and its treatment is fast-moving, the list of resources in the back of the book includes some websites that may help you find new and better ways to manage your bipolar symptoms. You can discuss the information you find on these sites with your mental health care provider. You can also visit my website, http://bipolar-101.blogspot.com, for the latest scientific findings on bipolar disorder, written for a lay audience. Stay informed, stay on track, and stay well.

A BIPOLAR RELAPSE PREVENTION CONTRACT

As in my first book, in this introduction I am including a contract that you can sign, as a commitment to yourself to take the steps you need to take to stay well. For each person, these steps will be different. Perhaps you are already doing most of what it takes and you just need to work on one area. Whatever it is that you need to do, putting it in writing will help you maintain a focus on your relapse prevention goal(s). You can copy this contract and place it in your wallet, on your bathroom mirror, or on your cell phone (for example by writing it in the notes utility on your phone) to keep you motivated and remind you what you need to do to stay well. If you are keeping a journal (which I highly recommend), putting your contract in the front of your journal is also a way to remind you of why you are keeping a journal.

 I, _____ (*your name*), will find the steps that work best for me to prevent bipolar relapse. I will create a plan, and I will follow that plan while monitoring and tracking my triggers, my bipolar symptoms, and my progress in each area (sleep, nutrition, activity, people). If I begin to experience symptoms, I will speak with my mental health care provider and seek out my support system for help. If I feel that I may be a danger to myself or other people, I promise to call a crisis hotline, 911, or my mental health care provider.

Signed _____
      (*signature*)

in _____ on _____ .
  (*city*)   (*date*)

CHAPTER 1

MEDICATION

There is no clear answer to the question "What causes bipolar disorder?" However, various brain imaging techniques have found differences in the brains of people with bipolar disorder and those without bipolar disorder. Bipolar disorder is rooted in variations in the transmission of nerve impulses in the brain, and because nerve impulses are managed by various neurochemicals, the source of this illness is widely accepted to be one that is related to biochemistry and neurochemistry in particular.

For this reason, medication is usually the first line of treatment. In fact, finding the right combination of medications and continuing to take them even when you are feeling well is crucial to success in treating your bipolar disorder. Along with therapy and education about the illness, medication is key to living well with bipolar disorder.

TYPES OF MEDICATION

Medications for bipolar disorder include mood stabilizers, sleep medications, and antidepressants.

- **Mood stabilizers** are important because they allow you to live without the extreme mood swings that are the hallmark of bipolar disorder.

- **Sleep medications** are used to counter the sleep disorders that often accompany bipolar disorder, especially during episodes of mania or depression. As will be described in chapter 3, sleep is very important to mental well-being and mood stability.

- **Antidepressants** are used to keep low moods at bay and to reduce the likelihood of suicide, as well as to minimize health-related issues that are associated with depression.

- **Anti-convulsants** are now a standard medication used to treat bipolar disorder, and have also been successfully used to treat acute mania.

- **Anti-psychotics** are also commonly used in maintenance treatment of bipolar disorder as well as with patients with acute mania and those experiencing psychotic symptoms.

Finding the medication(s) that will work for you over the long term often involves a lot of trial and error and requires you to cooperate closely with your mental health care provider. It also requires a lot of patience on your part. Sometimes finding and maintaining a good level of medication effectiveness with minimal side effects requires frequent adjustment of your dosages. At other times, you may need to switch medications because of problematic side effects or because a medication that once was effective for you is no longer effective. This process can be frustrating and time consuming. Taking medications also requires close monitoring by your mental health care provider. Because of all these reasons and more (see below), you may be tempted to take matters into your own hands by stopping one or more of your medications or taking it differently than prescribed.

STICKING TO YOUR MEDICATION

Because medicating mental illness is not an exact science, the best course of action is to take your medications as prescribed, unless the side effects are unmanageable, in which case you should talk to your prescriber. Monitoring the course of your bipolar disorder while you are on medication may prove that although you may have a mood episode here and there, you are most likely better off with medications than you are without them. That should be reason enough to keep taking them. You want to be well, and being well most of the time is better than being ill most of the time.

Therefore, once you find a drug combination that works, it is worth the effort to adhere to the dosage and timing of your medication regimen, to monitor for side effects, and to keep in close contact with your health care providers and notify them if side effects develop or worsen or if the effectiveness of any of your medications seems to change.

WHAT IS MEDICATION NON-ADHERENCE?

Non-adherence means not taking your medications as prescribed. Not taking your medications as prescribed can have a negative impact on your mental health and increase the likelihood of relapse.

Non-adherence includes:

- Not filling or refilling a prescription

- Stopping medications during treatment or against doctor's recommendation

- Taking more or less of a medication than is prescribed

- Taking a medication with contraindicated substances

- Taking a dose of medication at the wrong time

Importantly, taking medication as prescribed means following the guidelines for timing, dosage, and frequency. If medications are not taken as prescribed, they can lose their efficacy.

For people living with bipolar disorder, the EMBLEM study in Europe (Hong et al. 2011) found that of the 134 patients in the study,

23.6 percent were non-adherent over 21 months. This non-adherence was associated with a lower likelihood of remission and recovery, an increased risk of relapse and recurrence, and an increase in hospitalization and suicide attempts. It also had economic implications for the cost of care: non-adherence to medications for bipolar disorder results in higher health care expenditures over the long term for things like hospitalizations.

According to the National Consumers League (2011), almost three out of four Americans admit to not taking their medications as prescribed. Non-adherence to medications in general is such a problem that many major health care organizations, such as the Centers for Disease Control and Prevention (CDC), and major pharmaceutical companies are developing education and behavioral strategies to address it in an attempt to reduce its interference with the treatment of illnesses.

REASONS FOR MEDICATION NON-ADHERENCE

According to the World Health Organization (2003), there are five categories of factors that influence whether people take their medication as prescribed: economic and social factors, health care system factors, condition-related factors, therapy-related factors, and patient-related factors. Let us look at these factors as they relate to bipolar disorder.

Economic and Social Factors

With regard to *economic factors*, not having health insurance can be a significant barrier to getting the medications you need to treat your bipolar disorder. Sometimes medications can be very expensive, and if you have no consistent source of income, or not enough income, it may be difficult to be consistent with your medications. Sometimes it is difficult to get and maintain a job due to bipolar symptoms, and this makes it even harder to get and stay well.

Social factors include not having social support for taking medications. In some cultures and subcultures (such as the military), taking medications for mental health implies a moral or constitutional "weakness." There is also social stigma against mental illness, and you may not want to admit to yourself or others that you have a mental illness by taking medications for it. Social factors also include not having an environment that allows you to take medications when prescribed and that is conducive to allowing for side effects. For example, some medications make you sleepy, and that may interfere with your work performance to the point where you may have to change jobs or go on disability.

Health Care System Factors

Health care system factors include uncoordinated systems of care in which the patient has to negotiate between different practitioners who do not communicate with each other. Because people often seek care when they are most vulnerable, this is sometimes a barrier to treatment when people are most in need of help. Also, some insurance schemes make it a challenge to find a mental health care provider because there are gatekeepers who must make referrals to a provider, which lengthens the time between seeking help and getting help. A study conducted by a partnership of University of California–San Francisco (UCSF), San Francisco General Hospital, and Kaiser Permanente (a health management organization—HMO) revealed that a key factor in medication non-adherence in the United States was poor communication between medical providers and patients (Ratanawongsa et al. 2013).

Condition-Related Factors

Besides the fact that being depressed makes people unlikely to stick to the discipline of a medication routine, people with bipolar disorder who relapse into depression may feel that the fact that they relapsed means that their medication was ineffective, so they do not see the point in continuing it. In addition, feeling hopeless is an inherent symptom of depression. This hopelessness may decrease your motivation for taking medications because you feel powerless to make any changes in your health.

Alternatively, being hypomanic or manic may make people feel like they do not need any medication because they feel good. Because hypomania can make people feel productive, elated, and more at ease in social situations, they often choose not to medicate these feelings away and so can risk relapse by not adhering to their medication regimen.

Therapy-Related Factors

Therapy-related factors include some of the problematic side effects of bipolar medications, which include negative impacts on kidney and liver functioning, excessive sleepiness, hand tremors, and a wide range of other issues that often compete with the desire to take medications that are a key part of an overall treatment plan. Sometimes it may feel like you are choosing between your pancreas and your brain, or your liver or your brain, and these are tough choices to make. Many bipolar medications require quarterly (at least) blood draws to check your liver, kidney, and thyroid functioning, involving visits to clinics that would not be necessary if you were not taking these medications. Furthermore, the more drugs you have to take and the more complicated the timing of dosing, the more likely you are to forget taking a particular dose of a particular medication.

Sometimes it is necessary to try new medications, and this can interfere with your mood as you adjust to the new medication and its side effects, if any.

Patient-Related Factors

Patient-related factors include not wanting to take medications because you are in denial about your illness or because you feel that you are somehow at fault or responsible for being ill. If you are someone who has a difficult time taking pills, taking them daily may present a personal challenge that you have to overcome in order to take medications consistently as prescribed. Or you may simply be very busy or forgetful and therefore miss or delay doses. One study found that using alcohol and illicit substances was associated with poor medication adherence in a group of people with bipolar disorder (Jónsdóttir et al. 2013).

OVERCOMING ECONOMIC AND SOCIAL FACTORS

One thing you can do to keep the cost of your medications down is always make sure your health care providers and pharmacy know that you would prefer generic alternatives to name-brand medications, if possible. This will save you the cost of branding, and the price may be significantly lower than the name-brand version, even though the manufacturing standards and effectiveness are the same. If your income is limited, ask your health care providers whether there are any opportunities for you to get medications for free or at reduced cost. Some pharmaceutical companies have programs to help provide low-income patients with the medications they need. However, if you still cannot afford the medications to treat your bipolar disorder, the SNAP strategies in this book will be even more important to help lower your risk of relapse.

Having friends and family who support you in taking medications as prescribed can help you stick to your medication. Educating others and yourself about bipolar disorder can help you challenge the cultural and social barriers to making the right choices that will lead to lower incidence and severity of mood episodes. Leaning on your support network when you are under stress or when something happens that disrupts your regular routine will help you stick with your medication regimen, stay well, and prevent relapse. Finally, certain jobs (such as those that allow for working from home) are more conducive to taking medications when prescribed without a negative consequence to your occupational performance.

OVERCOMING HEALTH CARE SYSTEM FACTORS

Building good communication with your mental health care provider requires trust that is based on a good relationship. It is therefore important that you find the right provider for you. The right provider is one who has good availability, welcomes your questions, explains clearly what you need to do to maintain your mental health, understands what you want from your treatment, and respects your choices.

You have to advocate on your own behalf with your mental health care provider, because your health and well-being depend on it. Make sure you understand what is going on with your body, what the possible side effects of your medication are, and how long you may need to take your medication before you see an improvement, because these are all significant issues that may influence whether or not you want to take your medication. For example, if you decide that the side effects of a medication are a problem for you, instead of simply not taking it as prescribed, explain to your provider what the problem is and advocate for another option. You may also want to participate in a drug trial and have to advocate for yourself to be included.

OVERCOMING CONDITION-RELATED FACTORS

Because bipolar disorder is episodic, people living with the illness often want to stop taking their medications when they are feeling well, but maintaining mental well-being means consistently taking medications as prescribed.

What about when you are not feeling well? If you relapse into depression, you may think that it was because your medication was not effective, and the truth is that sometimes medications for mental illnesses stop working. Other times, there are "breakthrough symptoms," symptoms of mental illness that occur even though your medications are mostly effective at keeping them in check. Because of the limited ability of science to understand and predict mental illness, it is unrealistic to expect that once you are on medication, all your symptoms will disappear. That said, some people find the right medications that prevent another mood episode for years and years. The important thing is to talk to your mental health care provider if you have concerns that your medication is not working before you make any changes to how or whether you take it. On the other hand, if you relapse into mania or hypomania, it may be very difficult to convince yourself that you need to stay on your course of treatment because you feel great, but it is worth the effort so that you do not have to be hospitalized in order to regain stability. Remember that the irrational thinking and extreme behaviors typical of episodes of untreated mania or hypomania can land you in the hospital or in a lot of debt, or have other negative impacts.

OVERCOMING THERAPY-RELATED FACTORS

If you work closely with your health care providers, you can coordinate the timing of dosages so that it works well with your life and with other medications that you may be taking.

Keep a medication log to monitor the effects of any new medications so that you can see how effective they are in treating your condition and what side effects may be attributed to them. This will help you be accountable to yourself about your medications and also will help your health care providers assess the effectiveness or suitability of medications that they have prescribed for you. A medication log can provide vital information about how a medication works (or does not work) for you.

Date	Mg per Dose	Times Daily	4/7	4/8	4/9	4/10	4/11	4/12	4/13
Name of Medication or Supplement					Doses Taken				
Lithium	300	4	4	4	4	4	4	4	4
Side Effects					Severity (1–5)				
Dry mouth				3	3		4		0
Mood					Intensity (1–4)				
Mania			1	1	3	1	2	1	1
Depression									
Other Drugs					Used/Quantity				
Alcohol			1					2	

A blank medication log follows on the next page. Use this tool to track what medications you take, how often you take them, and any side effects you experience. This will help you monitor the impact that the medications have on your illness, and it supports a regular medication schedule that allows the drugs to work as intended and help you avoid a relapse. Knowing that you are going to be keeping a record also makes you more likely to take your medications. If you develop side effects that affect how well you stick to your medications, then this is something for you to discuss with your mental health care provider.

Writing down the degree to which side effects interfere with your daily routine (where 1 = low interference and 5 = high interference) will help you make associations between dosing and negative side effects. If you did not experience a side effect on a particular day, write "0" or use some other mark to show that you did not simply forget to notice or record this side effect. Because drinking alcohol or coffee and using tobacco and non-prescribed drugs may influence the efficacy of medications or may be linked to side effects, it is important to also track these substances. You can use an X to show that you used a particular substance on a particular day, or you can be more accurate and write in how many alcoholic beverages, cups of coffee, cigarettes, and so on you had. You can use "0" or draw a line for none, rather than leaving the box blank.

Refer to the following chart (adapted from White and Preston 2009) to track the severity of your manic or depressed mood, when applicable, on the Weekly Medication Log, using a scale of 1 to 4. (This chart, as well as the Weekly Medication Log, can be downloaded from the publisher's website for this book at http://www.newharbinger .com/28814.)

MOOD RATING SCALE

Mania	Depression
1 = more energetic/productive; routine maintained	1 = usual routine *not affected much*
2 = *some* difficulty with goal-oriented activity	2 = functioning with *some* effort
3 = *great* difficulty with goal-oriented activity	3 = functioning with *great* effort
4 = incapacitated or hospitalized	4 = incapacitated or hospitalized

(Other tools in this book will also have you track your mood, so this may seem like duplication. However, it is important to directly link your mood with your medications, since stabilizing mood is the point of taking them. And because moods are at the heart of bipolar disorder, keeping track of them is an integral part of monitoring the forces that drive them, so it is better to sometimes track your mood in more than one place than to not track it at all.)

Track your new medications or new dosage for at least a month using the Weekly Medication Log, and then discuss your findings with your mental health care provider.

WEEKLY MEDICATION LOG

Date														
Name of Medication or Supplement	Mg per Dose	Times Daily	Doses Taken											
Side Effects			Severity (1–5)											
Mood			Intensity (1–4)											
Mania														
Depression														
Other Drugs			Used/Quantity											

OVERCOMING PATIENT-RELATED FACTORS

If you are taking several medications, sometimes figuring out and sticking to proper timing and dosing can be overwhelming, and finding a medication routine that supports health becomes a challenge. The following strategies may help you keep on track with your medications.

Simplify your medication regimen. Sometimes you can take multiple medications at the same time. For example, instead of taking lithium throughout the day, perhaps you can take your daily dose all at once—say, at night. Reducing the frequency of your dose reduces the difficulty of sticking to the routine. Be sure to ask your health care providers whether it is okay to combine doses in this way and/or take different medications at the same time.

Using a pill dispenser that suits the dosage and frequency of your medication regimen will also simplify your regimen by giving you some structure.

Use reminder strategies. Pill organizers, calendars, and smartphone applications such as Pill Reminder, Dosecast, and MedCoach are some options for reminding yourself to take your medication as prescribed. Posting your medication regimen on your refrigerator or on your bathroom mirror is a good strategy for keeping on track with your medications. Setting an alarm on your watch or your cell phone to remind you when to take your medications is also a simple way to provide structure to your medication regimen.

Reduce your pill burden. The more pills that you have to take, the more likely you are to forget to take them, and the more complex your medication regimen. Instead of taking three 400-mg pills, for example, perhaps you can get a prescription for two 600-mg pills. Taking fewer pills makes taking medication less burdensome. Asking for long-acting versions of your medications is another way to reduce the number of pills you have to take throughout the day.

Involve your support system. Having support for taking your medications will increase your likelihood of taking them as prescribed. For example, alcohol is contraindicated for many medications; having your friends support you in eliminating alcohol from your social routine means maximizing the effectiveness of your medication and reducing the likelihood of problematic side effects and a better night's sleep.

Manage side effects. Some side effects of psychotropic medications are weight gain, constipation, dry mouth, sexual problems, nausea, tremors, and liver or kidney problems. Your mental health care provider can help you develop strategies for addressing each of the side effects that you experience. For example, drinking a lot of fluids can minimize the negative impact of certain medications on your kidneys. Make sure to get your blood tests as required for any medications that you are taking, because these tests serve as an important monitoring tool that will help you know whether your medications are having a negative impact on your vital organs, such as your pancreas, liver, and kidneys.

If you can reduce the impact of side effects, it will increase the likelihood that you will take your medication consistently. Some side effects are much more problematic than others and may require a change in medication.

Always have medication on hand. Waiting until you are out of medication to refill a prescription makes it more likely that you will miss a dose. So be proactive and request a refill before you run out. If you can, get your prescriptions filled by mail so that they are delivered to your house; this way, you are more likely to have your medications when you need them. I also recommend that you always carry a small pillbox containing enough of your medications for one or two days so that in case you have an unplanned night away from home, you do not have to interrupt your medication regimen and risk having a relapse of bipolar symptoms the next day. When taking a planned trip, bring a pill organizer that has divisions for day and night, and bring enough of each prescription for an extra day or two, just in case you are on the road longer than planned due to delays or other causes.

Talk to your health care providers. Communicate with your health care providers about the effectiveness of your medication, the side effects you experience, or any behavioral changes you have made that may influence how effective your medications are. For example, quitting smoking, reducing your alcohol or caffeine consumption, and increasing the amount of exercise you get may all mean that you no longer have to take certain drugs as frequently or at the same doses—exercise may reduce your dependence on antidepressants, and eliminating alcohol and caffeine may reduce your dependence on sleep medications. Keeping in close contact with your health care providers will help them adjust your dosages as necessary to maintain a regimen that maximizes the functioning of your brain and body.

SUMMARY

Medication adherence is very important to preventing bipolar relapse, because medications address the biochemical roots of the disorder. Finding the right medications requires patience, close monitoring, and good communication with your health care providers. Once you have found the right combination of medications, it is important that you take them as prescribed so that they can work optimally to prevent bipolar symptoms and reduce your risk of bipolar relapse. Strategies that work to support your adherence to your medication regimen should be incorporated into your lifestyle so that they take less effort over time and become the good habits that support your mental health.

CHAPTER 2

TRACKING AND MONITORING YOUR TRIGGERS AND MOOD

Bipolar disorder has strong genetic components, which means that you may have an inherent propensity for the illness. However, environmental causes play a role as well. The onset of your bipolar disorder may have been triggered by a major life event that caused you stress. Similarly, subsequent episodes of hypomania, mania, or depression are often preceded by a life event or circumstance that "triggers" the episode. Some of these triggers may be related to lifestyle, such as:

- Alcohol use (which can trigger depression)

- Sleep deprivation (which can trigger mania)

- Caffeine or tobacco use (which can trigger mania)

- An irregular daily schedule, such as eating, sleeping, and working at different times each day (which can trigger either mania or depression)

- Use of illicit substances (with drugs like cocaine being more likely to trigger mania and tranquilizers being more likely to trigger depression)

- Antidepressants and any other medications that include stimulants, including over-the-counter cold medications, appetite suppressants, thyroid medication, corticosteroids (which can trigger mania or depression depending on the medication)

- Eating foods high in sugar or not having a healthy diet (which, apart from causing you to not feel your best physically, can trigger mania or depression depending on the kinds of foods you are or are not eating)

- Missing doses or misusing your prescription medications, supplements, or alternative medicines (whether for bipolar disorder or other illnesses) (which, depending on the medications or supplements, can trigger either mania or depression)

- Lack of exercise (which can trigger either mania or depression)

Some triggers may be circumstantial or environmental, such as:

- Menstruation (which affects each woman differently)

- Excessive stimulation (which is more likely to trigger mania)

- High levels of stress (which can trigger either mania or depression)

- Abnormal levels of thyroid hormones (which can trigger depression or mania)

- Change in seasons and its accompanying difference in amount of daylight (with mania more likely in the summer and depression more likely in the winter)

Manic or depressive episodes are often triggered by major life events that cause stress, depending on how stress affects you and how you cope with stress in your life. Stressful life events can include:

- Difficulty in personal relationships

- Getting married

- Going away to college

- The death of someone close to you

- Financial difficulties

- A change in employment, such as starting a new job or losing a job

- Moving, especially if it is to a new place without an established support system

- Divorce or loss of a romantic partner

- The birth or illness of a child

- Problems at school or work

Tracking your triggers and monitoring your mood are key strategies for preventing bipolar relapse and reducing the severity and frequency of any bipolar symptoms you experience. Knowing what your triggers are will help you avoid them and thus help you avoid symptoms and mood changes. Monitoring your mood will help you be aware of your mental health status and the influence that different environmental conditions and triggers have on you. Keeping track of your mood and triggers will help you with all the other strategies in this book because you will see the effect that each one has on your mental well-being, whether it be in the area of sleep, nutrition, exercise, or social interaction with the people in your life. For example, when you track your mood and monitor your triggers and medications, you can see how getting more exercise or sticking to your medication affects not only your mood but also your sleep patterns, and also how your sleep patterns influence your mood.

If you experience a trigger, you can take steps to stabilize your mood before you get off track. For example, you can use exercise of some kind and a good sleep routine to counteract the mental health impact of having a stressful day. Paying attention to the details of your day and recording them will help you recognize patterns that cause your mood to improve or worsen and may trigger a relapse. Knowing that you are experiencing triggers may also help your health care providers understand your illness and help you manage your bipolar symptoms and prevent relapse with psychotherapy, medication, or practical advice. The more information you have, the more detailed questions you can ask of your health care providers so that you can best understand your options and make the best treatment decision—one that not only gives you peace of mind, but also works with your lifestyle to prevent bipolar symptoms and relapse.

WHAT AND WHEN TO TRACK

Bipolar disorder is a mood disorder, so tracking your mood is the way you monitor the symptoms of your illness. When tracking your mood, you make note of the intensity of your mood and the events or conditions that are precursors to any changes in how you are feeling physically as well as psychologically and emotionally. When you monitor your mood, you will be able to keep relapse at bay by intervening before any changes in your mood get out of control.

Because sleep, nutrition, activity, friends or family, stress, biological changes (menses, headaches, weight gain or loss, etc.) all interact with your mood and are often triggers for mood changes, these are the factors in the chart that appear in this chapter. If you find that something that is not on the chart influences your mood, you may want to add that to the chart. That is fine. The chart is flexible and designed to be specific to you and your triggers and the behaviors and conditions that have the most impact on your experience of bipolar disorder. You need to become aware of the factors that trigger changes in your mood and track these, because they are different for everyone, just as the side effects or success of various medications or behavioral interventions are also different for everyone.

If you have never tracked your triggers and mood before, you should track them for at least a month so that you have a sense of the rhythms of your mood and how various factors influence how you feel. After you have a sense of what keeps you stable and what throws you off, you may want to track your mood when you think that you might experience triggers. For example, if you think that you might be headed into a particularly stressful period at work, you would want to track your mood so that you could prevent relapse with preventive strategies or treatment interventions during a time when you are at risk of having a mood episode. The information you gather will also help your health care providers and your friends and family support you in preventing relapse.

WEEKLY TRIGGERS AND MOOD CHART

The following is a completed example of a chart for tracking your triggers and mood, followed by instructions for each section. You can photocopy the blank chart that comes afterward, or you can create your own version of it. I highly recommend that you recreate this chart in a computer-based spreadsheet program so that you can add and subtract items as necessary and use graphing or data analysis to better understand the relationships between your mood and your triggers. This can help you see patterns you may not notice when you are looking at a chart full of data.

You can also download this chart from the publisher's website for this book: http://www.newharbinger.com/28814.

This chart should not cause you anxiety or be a burden, so customize it to fit your life. No matter how you use it, it will give you a better understanding of your illness. With this understanding, you will be able to work to minimize the frequency and intensity of your symptoms of bipolar disorder and find ways to deal with symptoms as they arise so that you can stay well and prevent relapse.

SAMPLE WEEKLY TRIGGERS AND MOOD CHART

Weekly Triggers and Mood Chart for the Week of 4/7/14 to 4/13/14									
Medication or Supplement	Dose (mg)	Times Daily	Mon.	Tue.	Wed.	Thur.	Fri.	Sat.	Sun.
Lithium	300	4	4	4	4	4	4	4	4
Clonazepam	5	2	2	2	2	2	2	2	2
Side Effects									
Dry mouth				X			X		
Triggers									
Hours of sleep			7	6	8	5	7	7	8
Alcohol and drug use			0	1	0	2	0	0	0
Stress (0 to 10)			2	3	2	8	1	2	1
Menstruation			X.	X	X	X	X		
Major life event (–10 to 10)							2		

Mood						
Mania (0 to 4)	0	0	0	1	0	2
Depression (0 to 4)	0	0	0	2	1	0
Mixed states	0	0	0	X	0	0
No. of mood changes	0	0	0	3	0	0
Other Symptoms (0 to 10)						
Anxiety	0	X	0	3	0	0
Healthy Behaviors						
Exercise	X	X	X	0	X	X

Write in your chart at the end of each day. Although it may seem somewhat overwhelming to track your mood and your triggers daily, once you get the hang of it, it should take you no more than five minutes. Use zeroes (instead of blanks) to remind yourself that you had no bipolar symptoms or did not participate in a particular activity and did not simply forget to track something.

MEDICATION OR SUPPLEMENT

In the first section of the chart, track your medications and side effects. Remember to list whatever side effects you may be experiencing and put an X on the date that you experienced each one. If you want to be more accurate in your recording of side effects, you may choose to rate the intensity of these effects on a scale of 0 to 10 with 0 being no experience of that side effect and 10 being an intolerable level. If weight gain is a side effect, you will want to track it by weighing yourself daily so that you know how much weight you are gaining and at what rate.

Although this may seem duplicative (i.e., you may be tracking your medications and other factors elsewhere as well), this chart is the most comprehensive one in the book and allows you to track various triggers and behaviors in one place. However, you may choose to monitor only those factors that are triggers for your illness as they appear in each chapter.

TRIGGERS: HOURS OF SLEEP

In this box, write the number of hours you slept the previous night (i.e., if you got six hours of sleep Monday night, 6 is what you would record on Tuesday, as shown).

TRIGGERS: ALCOHOL AND DRUG USE

Place an X in this box if you used drugs or alcohol on this particular day. You may want to be more precise and record how many drinks you had (1 drink = 12 oz. of beer, 4 oz. of wine, or 1.5 oz. of hard liquor). This will be especially useful if you already have substance use issues.

TRIGGERS: STRESS

In this box, rate your level of stress for the day on a scale of 0 to 10, with 10 being the most stressful day possible and 0 being a day of no stress at all.

TRIGGERS: MENSTRUATION

For women, put an X in this box if you were menstruating. Hormonal changes due to menstruation are often a trigger for depressive symptoms, even in women without bipolar disorder. However, many women experience no change in bipolar symptoms due to menstruation. By tracking your monthly cycle, you can see whether your menstrual period is preceded or accompanied by changes in your mood.

TRIGGERS: MAJOR LIFE EVENT

If you experienced a major life event (whether positive or negative—see the list of examples earlier in this chapter), place an X in this box. For more precise recording, you may choose to rate the impact this event had on your life by rating it from –10 to 10, with –10 being the most negative impact possible and 10 being the most positive. If this event had a significant impact on your life, you may want to write more about the event and how it made you feel in your journal or on a separate sheet of paper.

MOOD

If you experienced higher than usual energy or productivity at all, record this in the mania box—rate the greatest amount of difficulty you had with goal-oriented activity on a scale of 1 to 4, where 1 is slight difficulty or not much difference in routine and 4 is incapacitation or hospitalization due to mania. If you experienced lower than usual energy or productivity at all, record this in the depression box—rate how much more effort than usual was required for you to function on a scale of 1 to 4, where 1 is slightly more effort or not much difference in routine and 4 is incapacitation or hospitalization due to depression. If your mood was stable or balanced, place a 0 in both boxes. (This chart can be downloaded from the publisher's website for this book: http://www.newharbinger.com/28814.)

MOOD RATING SCALE

Mania	Depression
1 = more energetic/productive; routine maintained	1 = usual routine *not affected much*
2 = *some* difficulty with goal-oriented activity	2 = functioning with *some* effort
3 = *great* difficulty with goal-oriented activity	3 = functioning with *great* effort
4 = incapacitated or hospitalized	4 = incapacitated or hospitalized

MIXED STATES

Place an X in this box if you experienced mixed symptoms, which is when you have symptoms of depression and mania at the same time. Mixed symptoms often feel like agitation or irritability mixed with feelings of sadness.

NUMBER OF MOOD CHANGES

Record the number of mood changes you had on this particular day. You may have to estimate this number, as it is often difficult to keep track of mood changes while you are experiencing them.

OTHER SYMPTOMS

List other physical and mental symptoms of bipolar disorder that you experienced and place an X in the box for that day. You may choose to be more precise and rate the interference of these symptoms with your life on a scale of 1 to 10, with 1 being not very much and 10 being the most interference possible.

HEALTHY BEHAVIORS

You can use this part of the chart to track your exercise habits as described in chapter 5.

Weekly Triggers and Mood Chart for the Week of _____ to _____

Medication or Supplement	Dose (mg)	Times Daily	Mon.	Tue.	Wed.	Thur.	Fri.	Sat.	Sun.
Side Effects									
Triggers									
Hours of sleep									
Alcohol and drug use									
Stress (0 to 10)									
Menstruation									
Major life event (–10 to 10)									

Mood								
Mania (0 to 4)								
Depression (0 to 4)								
Mixed states								
No. of mood changes								
Other Symptoms (0 to 10)								
Healthy Behaviors								

CUSTOMIZING YOUR CHART

Feel free to customize your Weekly Triggers and Mood Chart to suit your needs with the factors that are specific to your bipolar disorder. The list of triggers that I listed earlier is a place to start, and you can add items as relevant or remove ones that are not relevant to you. This chart is the basis for a lifestyle in which you manage your illness to prevent relapse. It is a great source of information about your triggers, your behaviors, and your bipolar symptoms, and it will help you and your health care providers manage your triggers and mood to help you stay well and prevent relapse.

For example, if you know that you are prone to seasonal changes in your mood that tend to trigger mixed episodes, depression, or mania, and happen to observe daylight saving time, you may want to monitor your mood particularly closely in October and November, because when daylight saving time ends it may disrupt your body's sleep cycle. Taking early notice of a consistently low mood may help you intervene quickly to prevent relapse. By creating a customized chart that reflects your own triggers and symptoms of bipolar disorder, you will be able to come to a better understanding of how your bipolar disorder operates, and you can be more aware of potential issues that can cause relapse.

SUMMARY

Tracking and monitoring your mood and triggers will provide you with the information you need to take actions that will prevent bipolar relapse. You may not choose to monitor everything all the time, but understanding that changes in your behaviors or in the environment will have an impact on your mood allows you to prepare for risks to your mental health and to maintain behaviors and seek out environments that support your desire to prevent bipolar relapse.

CHAPTER 3

SLEEP

Sleep problems can be a symptom of bipolar disorder, and lack of sleep—due to any cause—can precipitate a mood episode (APA 2000). Getting good sleep is therefore both a way of preventing bipolar relapse and a way of knowing that you are not experiencing symptoms of your bipolar disorder. If your sleep is good, then you are most likely also in good mental health.

If you do not feel rested when you wake and are not productive, healthy, and happy; or if you are dependent on caffeine during the day; or if you feel sleepy in the afternoon or when driving, there are things you can do to improve your sleep. Even if you are already sleeping well, these same things can help you optimize the quality and quantity of your sleep and maintain your healthy sleep patterns. In this chapter, I will give you tips on "sleep hygiene." Sleep hygiene refers to behaviors that are associated with getting restful sleep. This includes things like having a set bedtime, drinking calming herbal tea before bed, and keeping the room in which you sleep cool and dark. I will also give you tools for monitoring and managing your sleep.

THE NEED FOR SLEEP

Sleep is important to everyone's health. It helps regulate your immune system and cardiovascular (circulatory system) function (Kerkhofs and Boudjeltia 2012). In a study of immune system response and sleep, researchers Charlene Gamaldo, Annum Shaikh, and Justin McArthur (2012) found a strong relationship between sleep and immunity function: sleep dysfunction was shown to increase the likelihood of infection and immune-related illnesses.

Unfortunately, according to the National Heart, Lung, and Blood Institute (NHLB; 2003), chronic sleep loss and sleep disorders may affect up to 70 million Americans (almost one-fourth of the population). Not only are sleep problems widespread, but they can be harmful and costly. Lack of sleep is a leading cause of accidents both on the road and on the job.

So what is the recommended amount of sleep per night? According to the National Sleep Foundation (2013), there is no "magic number" of hours of sleep. Each individual has different requirements based on his or her *basal sleep need*, which is the amount of sleep needed for optimal performance, and *sleep debt*, which is the amount of sleep that person has lost to illness, insomnia, and so forth. Although everyone has different sleep needs, the National Sleep Foundation suggests that most adults need between seven and nine hours of sleep to be at their best.

SLEEP AND BIPOLAR DISORDER

The *Diagnostic and Statistical Manual of Mental Disorders* (*DSM-S*; APA 2000) states that people with bipolar disorder are more likely to have problems sleeping. Sleep deficit is a trigger for depression, mania, and hypomania. Sleeplessness is a symptom of mania, and although depression often results in feeling tired, it can also lead to changes in sleep, which might result in either sleeplessness or sleeping too much. Not being able to sleep can also be a symptom of a mixed episode (in which you have symptoms of depression and mania at the same time). Sleep is thus a significant issue for mental well-being that should be monitored by people living with bipolar disorder.

People whose bipolar disorder has been diagnosed and is being successfully treated are less likely to have sleep problems. However, if you have sleep problems, your doctor may prescribe a medication that induces sleep (e.g., clonazepam, any other benzodiazepine, or zolpidem), to reduce your risk of a mood episode. Even if you are taking a sleep medication, good sleep hygiene may allow you and your mental health care provider to reduce the dosage of your sleep medication and also reduce your risk of the onset of bipolar symptoms, meaning you may not need as much of other medications either. A study of sleep deficit found that sleep management was an important factor in preventing depression in people with bipolar disorder (Perlman, Johnson, and Mellman 2006), and routine and sleep regularity have been found to reduce the onset of bipolar symptoms in general (Frank, Gonzalez, and Fagiolini 2006; Srinivasan et al. 2006).

GOOD SLEEP AND ITS BENEFITS

As outlined above, good sleep is essential for your health, just as are good nutrition (which we will discuss in chapter 4) and physical activity (chapter 5). You will know that you are getting good sleep when you are tired at bedtime, you fall asleep within thirty minutes, you stay asleep for six to eight hours, and you wake up feeling rested.

Without a good night's sleep, you may be more likely to have accidents, think less clearly, make poor decisions, and forget things. Getting the sleep you need supports healthy organ function, which reduces your risk of hypertension, diabetes, cardiovascular disease, and other illnesses.

Good sleep also gives your immune system some fighting power so that you can resist common infections like a cold or the flu. And good sleep puts you at lower risk for depression (Baglioni et al. 2011) and mania (Gruber et al. 2011). And good sleep may keep you slender (Spaeth, Dinges, and Goel 2013), which can be an issue for people who have to take antipsychotics and other medications, such as lithium and olanzapine, that may lead to weight gain.

CIRCADIAN RHYTHMS

A study of the relationship between circadian rhythms and bipolar disorder (McGrath et al. 2009) showed that people with bipolar disorder had a genetic mutation in an area critical to the production of a protein that regulates circadian rhythms. The findings indicate a possible explanation why sleep has such a strong relationship with bipolar disorder.

According to the National Institute of General Medical Sciences (NIGMS; 2013), circadian rhythms are the physical, behavioral, and mental changes that follow the natural cycle of light and dark over the course of a day (twenty-four hours). Most living things have circadian rhythms, and humans are no different. Our circadian rhythms are driven by our internal biological clocks and some external factors, like temperature and light, and are influenced by genetics. Circadian rhythms are important to your sleep patterns because your body's "master clock" controls the production of melatonin, a hormone that makes you sleepy. Your master clock is regulated by light, and when your body perceives less light, there is a higher production of melatonin to make you sleepy. Research in this area may lead to treatments for sleep disorders that may be important to the treatment of bipolar disorder because sleep disturbance is such a significant symptom of the illness for so many people.

INSOMNIA

Insomnia, the most common sleep complaint, is defined as trouble falling asleep, difficulty staying asleep, waking too early, or not feeling rested in the morning even if you have had an opportunity to have good sleep (American Academy of Sleep Medicine 2012a). The occasional nighttime tossing and turning does not constitute insomnia.

Insomnia is usually associated with stress; medical conditions; mental disorders (e.g., bipolar disorder); certain medications such as antidepressants, which can also cause manic symptoms (Silverstone and Silverstone 2004); substance use or abuse; environmental factors (e.g., noise, light, or extreme temperatures); and habits or lifestyles (e.g., shift work).

Insomnia may result in the following symptoms (American Academy of Sleep Medicine 2012b):

- Daytime sleepiness

- Worry or frustration about sleep

- Cognitive impairment as evidenced by problems with attention, memory, or concentration

- Extreme mood changes or irritability

- Lack of energy or motivation

- Poor performance at school or work

- Tension headaches or stomachaches

The impact of insomnia on people living with bipolar disorder includes, as mentioned, an increased risk of bipolar symptoms. Insomnia is both a symptom of bipolar disorder and a cause of bipolar relapse, so it is important to understand what may cause it and how it influences your mental health. Insomnia can be caused by poor sleep hygiene, which includes the following:

- Too much activity before bedtime, which includes mental activities such as problem solving or physical activity such as dancing or working out

- Doing activities in bed other than sleeping (reading, watching television, working on a laptop, playing video games, writing, texting, instant messaging, etc.)

- Using substances that disturb your sleep (tobacco, alcohol, caffeine, etc.) (Some experts suggest not using these substances close to bedtime, or or eliminating them entirely.)

- Taking naps

BEATING INSOMNIA

The UK's National Health Service (NHS Choices 2012) provides the following ten tips for beating insomnia (for which it cites the Sleep Council).

KEEPING REGULAR HOURS

Keeping regular hours means going to sleep and waking at the same time each day, even on weekends. As a guideline, your bedtime should be determined by how much sleep you need to get to feel rested the next day. For example, if you need to wake at seven most mornings, and you have found that you do not feel rested if you get less than eight hours of sleep, give yourself an eleven o'clock bedtime. Go to bed at this time seven days a week—don't stay up late even if you are not sleepy or can sleep in the next day. Going to bed at a specific time each night even if you are not sleepy will help your body get into a rhythm of becoming tired at this bedtime. This gets your body's circadian rhythms in synchronicity, meaning that your body gets into a pattern of sleeping and waking that regulates itself, and your body will then want to wake at the same time every morning because it will be getting the amount of sleep it needs.

Regular sleep is good for maintaining a balanced mood. Taking naps interferes with your sleep regularity, so avoid them, especially in the late afternoon—a late-afternoon nap may leave you too alert to fall asleep at night.

Expose yourself to daylight during the day. Some people with insomnia may have co-occurring seasonal affective disorder that may best be treated with bright light therapy (discuss this with your mental health care provider). Exposure to daylight during the day, especially upon waking, has been shown to have a strong impact on regulating circadian rhythms, which is important to mood stability (NIGMS 2013).

If you take medications at bedtime, taking them at the same time each night will also allow them to take effect at a consistent time and support your sleep routine. If they are fast-acting you should take them closer to bedtime, and if they are long-acting you should take them earlier so that they take effect when you are ready to sleep.

Have a bedtime routine that includes things like brushing your teeth, as well as relaxing activities (see "Relax Before Going to Bed" later in this chapter), and start this routine at the same time each night. When you first begin to keep regular hours, your life may feel overly regimented, but eventually it will become a healthy habit that helps you get the best sleep you can get each night.

CREATE A RESTFUL SLEEP ENVIRONMENT

A dark, cool room provides the optimal environment for restful sleep. If there are bright lights outside your window at night, if there is an annoying indoor light (e.g., from a computer or electronic thermostat), or if you sleep during daylight hours, you may require the use of a blindfold to "fool" your brain into thinking that it is dark. Noise should also be at a minimum, or perhaps you respond well to soothing music or sounds. If you need quiet, then a pair of earplugs may be a great investment that pays valuable sleep dividends. Remove any items from your sleep environment that may create stress—your clock, for example, if you tend to watch the clock once you are in bed. If you need an alarm, you can move the clock to another room or cover it so that you cannot see it but it is still close enough for you to hear and turn off. It is also good not to look at the clock if you wake in the middle of the night, because this may create anxiety that interferes with your body's ability to return to sleep.

Creating a restful sleep environment also means not using your bed for activities like writing, using your laptop, or watching television; the fewer distractions, the better. If you have a pet that makes noise during the night or disrupts your sleep in any way, it would be best to find alternate sleep arrangements for the pet so that you can get the high-quality sleep that makes you less susceptible to relapse. If you are the parent of a child who has difficulty falling asleep or often wakes up at night (which can affect your own sleep), you can use the same sleep hygiene tips in this chapter to help him or her get better sleep too. For example, make sure your child gets lots of physical activity each day, sticks to a nightly sleep routine, avoids meals near bedtime, and keeps his or her bedroom cool and dark. (If your child uses a night light, you can turn it off after he or she falls asleep so that if your child wakes the light does not make it harder for him or her to return to sleep.)

Other things that can make for a restful sleep environment are the use of scented candles, especially lavender, which is very soothing and calming. To make sure that you do not fall asleep with them still burning, you can light candles and dim the lights as you get ready for bed, then blow out the candles before getting into bed. Dimming the lights as you begin your bedtime routine, along with the calming candlelight, can get you in the right frame of mind for sleep.

MAKE SURE THAT YOU ARE IN A COMFORTABLE BED

A comfortable bed is part of a restful sleep environment but is specific to your ability to fall asleep and stay asleep. Your bed should be as hard or as soft as you need for sleeping. Your sheets and pillows and sleep clothes should also be comfortable, which means that your linens should be clean and soft—you may not realize that rough or unwashed fabrics are irritating your skin and making it hard to sleep. Make sure that you are not allergic to anything in your linens or your mattress. Common allergens include down, petrochemicals, flame retardants and other additives such as formaldehyde, and dust mites (tiny bugs that live in mattresses and pillows and require special treatment). Symptoms of allergies may include sneezing, itching, a rash, or a runny nose. Your pillows should be hypoallergenic if necessary and of a firmness that provides the support and the comfort that your body prefers.

Lying in your bed should make you want to fall asleep, so investment in a mattress that fits your personal preferences in physical comfort is well worth it. If you think that your mattress may be the problem, then take your time shopping for a new mattress by trying different ones until you find the one that is most comfortable for you. A good night's sleep that leads to a more stable mood and a day spent bright and alert is worth the time and money it may take to find the mattress that is right for you.

EXERCISE REGULARLY

The National Institutes of Health (NIH; n.d.) recommends moderate exercise for 150 minutes each week; you can make this target easily by doing thirty minutes of exercise at least five days per week (for more on exercise, see chapter 5). For people with bipolar disorder it is particularly effective to exercise in the morning: it helps you have a clear head during the day. Getting exercise during your day also increases the likelihood that you will fall asleep quickly when you go to bed at night and improves the quality of your sleep. It is best to finish exercising no later than three hours before your bedtime, however, because it sometimes takes this long for your metabolism, body temperature, heart rate, and brain activity to return to levels that are conducive to sleep.

LESS CAFFEINE

Caffeinated products such as tea, coffee, cocoa, chocolate, and sodas deter sleep (Júdice et al. 2013) and have a negative impact on the quality of sleep, particularly if they are ingested in the afternoon or evening. Because caffeine's effects can last up to twenty-four hours, its impact on sleep can be significant. If you find it hard to eliminate caffeine altogether, then a good rule is to not have any caffeine after noon or at least any later than four hours before your bedtime. Instead, drink herbal teas that induce sleep, such as chamomile. Warm milk or any drink made with milk or yogurt—such as a smoothie—contains the amino acid tryptophan, which facilitates sleep. Avoid drinds like chocolate milk, hot chocolate, or hot cocoa; while they may make you feel sleepy, the caffeine in the chocolate may interfere with actually falling asleep.

DON'T OVERINDULGE

Too much food or alcohol will make it hard for your body to fall asleep and stay asleep. If your body is working on digesting food, this will make it harder for you to fall asleep. It is best to eat your last meal of the day two hours before going to bed; if you are hungry after that, have a light snack, such as crackers, warm milk, or fruit. Alcohol may help you fall asleep, but it reduces the quality of your sleep by interrupting REM sleep. REM sleep (REM stands for rapid eye movement, due to the eyeball twitching that is often observed in those in this stage of sleep) is when most dreams occur and is important to learning new mental skills (National Institute of Neurological Disorders and Stroke 2007). Drinking alcohol before bedtime also makes you more likely to wake up during the night.

DON'T SMOKE

Nicotine is a stimulant, and smoking creates a poor physical environment for sleep. According to the National Institute of Neurological Disorders and Stroke (2007), smoking delays the onset of sleep, reduces REM sleep, and makes you more likely to wake in the middle of the night. Nicotine can also cause nightmares. Of course, smoking has other negative health impacts, so this is a good place to start to make a change.

RELAX BEFORE GOING TO BED

Create a bedtime routine that begins about an hour before your bedtime. For example, you could start by taking your prescribedmedications (in particular, those medications that make you drowsy) so that they have some time to take effect before you get into bed. (If the medications that make you drowsy work quickly, you may want to take them last. Avoid over-the-counter sleep medications unless you have consulted with your mental health care provider.) Then do something that relaxes you. A calming activity like yoga or meditation works to relax your body, clear your thoughts, and put you in a peaceful frame of mind. Some people like to take a warm bath or shower; others like to read a book in their favorite chair. What one person finds relaxing, another may find stimulating or invigorating, so find the activity or activities that work best for you.

Although you may enjoy watching TV before bed, it is generally not a good way to relax, because your mind will be too active to fall asleep and the bright light from the screen may keep your body awake for longer. Instead, try listening to some soothing music by candlelight. Also, do not indulge in any activity that may be stressful or stimulating, such as playing competitive games, working, paying bills, or problem solving, before bed.

Whatever you do to relax, be sure to do it out of bed, and in another room if possible. Reserving your bed for sleep and intimacy will teach your body to associate your bed with sleeping, and you will eventually fall asleep more quickly.

The last part of your bedtime routine should include the necessary tasks, such as brushing your teeth, washing your face, and taking your (quick-acting) medications. It may sound simple, but urinating right before bed decreases the likelihood of needing to get up in the middle of the night to make a trip to the bathroom. This is important if you drink fluids with your medications or if you take a diuretic like lithium, which may cause you to frequently urinate and thus disrupt your sleep.

Get into bed fifteen to thirty minutes before your bedtime so that your mind and body can relax and get comfortable. The point is to slow down your mind and body so that they are ready for sleep. Make sure that you have set your alarm and put a glass of water by the bed. (Medications such as lithium can cause dehydration, and if you wake up thirsty in the middle of the night, a quick sip or two of water can be a quick way to get back to sleep without fully waking.) Some people find it works to listen to quiet music or a special CD or playlist of restful sounds at this time, while others prefer silence. If you are one of the latter, then you may want to sleep with earplugs. Avoid doing anything in bed that may be stimulating, such as watching television, texting, or playing games on a device. Instead, just close your eyes and settle in.

WRITE AWAY YOUR WORRIES

Worrying about what you need to do tomorrow may keep you lying awake at night, so take the time to make a list of what you need to do so that you can clear it from your mind. You may also want to prepare for the next day by putting out your clothes and shoes and making sure that your keys, umbrella, briefcase, laptop, phone, and so on are in a set place, which will help you feel more prepared for the next day. Keeping a journal, as suggested in chapter 2, may also help you clear your mind and is a great tool for tracking your emotions and your mood.

DON'T WORRY IN BED

Sometimes no matter what you do to relax before bedtime, worry still has you lying in bed staring at the ceiling. If that occurs, get up and do something relaxing—a stretch, a yoga pose, meditation, reading—or make yourself some warm milk or relaxing herbal tea. Make sure that your room is cool and dark, and set the ringer on your phone to silent (or turn your phone off completely) in order to minimize distractions. Then return to bed when you feel sleepy.

MONITORING AND TRACKING YOUR SLEEP

If you suffer from insomnia, monitoring and tracking your sleep will help you find out what may be causing you to have poor sleep. It will also show you what you are doing that promotes good sleep so that you can do those things more often.

Even if you do not suffer from insomnia, before a mood episode begins or early in a mood episode (relapse), you may experience a change in your sleep patterns, whether in the quantity (number of hours) or the quality of your sleep. For example, you may wake frequently during the night, or you may not feel rested when you get out of bed and begin your day. Being aware of these changes and recording them and the behaviors that accompany them will help you and your health care providers take steps to either prevent an episode or mediate its length and severity through changes in behaviors that influence sleep.

Monitoring the number of hours you slept is something that you will do on a regular basis with the Weekly Triggers and Mood Chart in chapter 2. However, when you are having difficulties with sleep—either too much or too little—you can keep a detailed sleep log (or "sleep diary") to be better able to monitor your sleep, understand the nature of your difficulties, and track your progress in trying to make changes to your sleep routine and changes to your habits that may affect your sleep. Here is a simple sleep log that may work for you. It is a chart that tracks your sleep and your mood.

SAMPLE WEEKLY SLEEP LOG

Date	Mood (M, D, MS)	Time You Went to Bed (p.m.)	Time You Fell Asleep	Morning Wake Time (a.m.)	Hours of Sleep	Quality of Sleep/Number of Times You Woke During the Night
9/26/13		10:00	Unsure	6:00	8	Excellent
9/27/13	1D	11:00	11:30	6:00	6.5	Okay/Woke once
9/28/13		10:30	10:45	6:00	7.25	Good
9/29/13		11:00	11:30	6:00	6.5	Good
9/30/13	1D	11:45	Midnight	6:30	6.5	Okay
9/31/13		11:00	11:15	6:00	6.75	Good
10/01/13		11:00	11:15	6:00	6.75	Great

You can photocopy the following blank sleep log, make your own version, or download or print it from the publisher's website for this book at http://www.newharbinger.com/28814. Fill it in shortly after you wake up, following these steps:

1. Write today's date.

2. Using the Mood Rating Scale in chapter 2, rate your level of depression or mania and place the letter D or M next to the number accordingly. If you're experiencing mixed states, use the letters MS. If your mood is stable, you may leave the box blank.

3. Record the time you went to bed last night.

4. Record the time you fell asleep last night. (You will probably need to estimate, especially if, as suggested, you don't watch the clock.)

5. Record the time you got out of bed today.

6. Calculate the number of hours you slept by determining how long it was between the time you fell asleep and the time you woke.

7. Grade the quality of your sleep as excellent, good, okay, bad, or very bad. Alternatively, record the number of times you woke up in the middle of the night, which is also an indicator of sleep quality. (You may need to estimate, because your memory may be hazy.)

WEEKLY SLEEP LOG

Date	Mood (M, D, MS)	Time You Went to Bed (p.m.)	Time You Fell Asleep	Morning Wake Time (a.m.)	Hours of Sleep	Quality of Sleep/Number of Times You Woke During the Night

Following is a descriptive list of other sleep logs available online. Each log has its own unique strengths, and you can try one or more of them and choose the one that suits you best. Use whichever log you choose on a daily basis to track your sleep as well as your triggers for insomnia and mood disregulation, such as alcohol, caffeine, and street drugs, and other factors that affect your sleep. Once you find a sleep routine that works for you and you are consistently getting good sleep, then you may choose to use sleep monitoring tools only as needed, depending on your own assessment of risk, such as increased stress or change in seasons.

- The UK's National Health Service's "Daily Sleep Diary" (http://www.nhs.uk/livewell/insomnia/documents/sleep diary.pdf)

  This very straightforward one-page diary is for seven days and monitors sleep only. It has you track what time you go to bed, what time you wake up, and how long it takes you to fall asleep, as well as the quality of your sleep. It would be a good starter diary for you to see whether you are getting enough sleep. But because it does not monitor triggers for insomnia, it does not help with figuring out what the sources of any sleep problems may be.

- Patient.co.uk's "Sleep Diary" (http://patient.co.uk/health/sleep-diary.htm)

  This diary is three pages long, poses nineteen questions, and covers a two-week period. It is highly detailed and includes units of alcohol and caffeine taken before and after 5:00 p.m., exercise before and after 9:00 p.m., naps, quality of sleep, and whether you took any street drugs. It is the most detailed of the diaries listed here and is the one that requires you to be most diligent and consistent. However, it will also provide the most detailed information and support you greatly in making specific changes to your routine that may improve your sleep. Because it includes the use of alcohol, caffeine, and street drugs, this diary would also be a very useful tool for your mental health care provider if you are having problems that are not related to sleep but may be contributing to other bipolar symptoms.

- Helpguide.org's "Weekly Sleep Diary" (http://www.helpguide.org/life/pdfs/sleep_diary.pdf)

     This weekly two-page diary covers a lot of territory. It includes exercise, alcohol and caffeine, feelings, food and drink, medications and sleep aids, bedtime routine, quality of sleep, hours of sleep, and any sleep breaks. This will provide you with comprehensive information about your sleep habits and about your behaviors and habits that inhibit or facilitate good sleep hygiene.

- The National Sleep Foundation's "National Sleep Foundation Sleep Diary" (http://sleep.buffalo.edu/sleepdiary.pdf)

     This sleep diary uses checkboxes to track your exercise, caffeine intake, alcohol intake, medications, and sleep routine, as well as the quantity and quality of your sleep. Though it is two pages long for each week, it is thorough and very easy to use. It has one part to be completed in the morning and one part to be completed at night.

- The Center for Sleep and Wake Disorders' "Sleep Log/Diary" (http://www.sleepdoc.com/pdf/sleep_log.pdf)

     This twenty-eight-day journal is simple to use, because it tracks your activity using a brief code. It includes a graph with boxes that cover one-hour periods in which you place a code to indicate when you went to bed, when you were asleep, when you got out of bed, when you ate, when you took your medication, when you exercised, and when you watched TV. It does better with tracking the frequency or quantity of factors that may affect your sleep than the quality of that factor. For example, there is a code for caffeine but no guideline for indicating how much, and the same goes for food. However, it is easy for people of all ages to use and provides graphical information. It also includes a comment section for you to add any details you want to.

It is very difficult indeed to change all your bad habits at once, so once you find out which factors and behaviors are negatively influencing your sleep, choose one thing to work on at a time. Perhaps your caffeine habit is getting in the way. Start by reducing your intake of caffeinated beverages by one cup a day or by stopping your intake at a certain time, such as noon. You may find that is enough to bring your sleep in line with what you need. Work at different behaviors in the same way, and you will develop a new set of habits that become a part of your life and make lack of sleep less of a trigger for your bipolar symptoms.

If monitoring and tracking your sleep and making changes in your behavior do not result in more hours of sleep and better-quality sleep, then make an appointment with your mental health care provider and bring your sleep log with you so that together you can assess what other strategies you may need to implement. This may include the addition of sleep medications to your medication regimen, or a change in sleep medications if you are already taking medications for sleep. If your sleep problems are chronic and last for more than a week without any apparent direct cause (e.g., new meds, stress, or other changes in your life), you may want to discuss the possibility of getting assessed for a co-occurring sleep disorder, such as insomnia or sleep apnea.

HOW TO FIND OUT MORE

If you want to know more about sleep and mental well-being and find evidence-based strategies for improving sleep, the UK's Mental Health Foundation offers a free e-book on sleep, called *Sleep Matters: The Impact of Sleep on Health and Wellbeing*, at http://www.mentalhealth .org.uk/publications/sleep-report. The National Heart, Lung, and Blood Institute has a free sleep guide called *Your Guide to Healthy*

Sleep at http://www.nhlbi.nih.gov/health/public/sleep/healthysleepfs .pdf. The National Sleep Foundation (http://www.sleepfoundation .org) and the American Academy of Sleep Medicine (http://sleepedu cation.com) also provide a lot of useful and easily accessible information.

If after trying many of the steps outlined in this chapter, you still have trouble sleeping, then see your mental health care provider or contact a sleep clinic, if there is one in your area. A good place to start is the American Academy of Sleep Medicine's consumer website which has a "Find a Sleep Center" tool: http://www.sleepeducation.com /find-a-center.

SUMMARY

Good sleep is the first part of the SNAP approach to preventing bipolar relapse that is the heart of this book. Because of the significance of poor sleep as a symptom of both mania and depression and its function as a trigger for both of these conditions, getting good sleep is probably the most important thing you can do to prevent bipolar relapse. Understanding why you may not be getting a good night's sleep and finding ways to get restful sleep is a good foundation to help you maintain your mental well-being and keep your mood steady.

CHAPTER 4

NUTRITION

Experimental and clinical evidence indicates that an appropriate diet can reduce the symptoms of bipolar disorder, especially the symptoms of depression. Your body and brain need the right nutrients to work their best, but eating regularly and healthily can be a challenge in a fast-food, processed-food world.

To help you keep track of your eating habits and your nutritional intake, there will be several tracking and monitoring tools offered in this chapter. Not all tools work for all people, and you can modify these tools to suit your own needs. These tools will also be available on the publisher's website for this book at http://www.newharbinger.com /28814.

THE IMPORTANCE OF GOOD NUTRITION FOR YOUR MENTAL AND PHYSICAL HEALTH

Higher intake of nutrients is associated with higher levels of overall mental functioning (Davidson and Kaplan 2012). This may mean that the better your diet, the better your brain will function. (Your body will also function a lot better too.) The better your brain functions, in turn, the less likely you are to have a mood episode, while nutritional deficits or the poor health that comes from poor nutrition may trigger just such an episode.

Good nutrition helps your body cope with stress, and people with bipolar disorder need to maximize their body's ability to deal with stress so that episodes of mania or depression are not triggered. Good nutrition builds a strong immune system. It also helps your body resist the effects of aging. Good nutrition also can minimize the effects of chronic illness, which often is a trigger for depression. At the very least, if your body feels good, you are more likely to feel good as well.

Your body needs vitamins, iron, iodine, and other trace elements to make hormones and enzymes and to help your cells, tissues, and organs do their jobs. Because you only need tiny amounts of these substances, they are known as micronutrients. Certain micronutrients such as vitamin D are essential to your mental well-being (Khamba et al. 2011).

Overall, good nutrition gives your brain the fuel it needs to function well. It helps you think clearly and coherently, it helps stabilize your mood, it promotes a healthy response to stress, and it supports your ability to carry out your daily tasks, whether they be making statistical calculations or planning a wedding. Eating well is the key to preventing chronic health conditions such as type 2 diabetes (which can be due to eating too much processed sugars), stroke (which is due to eating too much bad cholesterol), and heart disease. These chronic illnesses can trigger bipolar symptoms due both to the chemical imbalances that they create and the ongoing stress that they can cause.

CO-OCCURRING EATING DISORDERS

If you have an eating disorder, such as anorexia, overeating, or bulimia, in addition to bipolar disorder, it requires special management by your mental health care provider. Stress may trigger both the symptoms of eating disorders and the symptoms of bipolar disorder. If you are not eating enough, or if you are purging, lack of certain vitamins and other micronutrients can stress your brain and the body and increase the likelihood of bipolar relapse, because your body—and mind—will not have the nutrients it needs to function properly.

Even in the absence of an eating disorder, some people eat in unhealthy ways when they are experiencing the early onset of bipolar symptoms. For example, when some people are depressed they may eat too much or not at all, and people who are manic often have a reduced appetite. The tools in this chapter will help you keep track of your eating and your associated moods so that you can be aware of how your eating habits may trigger a mood episode or can clue you in to the early onset of a relapse so that you can intervene as early as possible.

EATING WELL WITH BIPOLAR DISORDER

Because eating healthily can improve your overall physical and mental health, we will focus for the most part on general nutrition and then turn to topics that pertain specifically to bipolar disorder. Good general nutrition is the baseline everyone needs for optimal brain functioning and mood regulation and is particularly important for buttressing your brain against environmental or nutritional triggers for your bipolar disorder.

If you want to eat well, you must educate yourself on the key principles of good nutrition. Reading this chapter will help you understand good nutrition, but you may also want to visit the US Department of Agriculture's nutrition website at http://www.choosemyplate.gov. This website features advice for eating healthy on a budget, sample menus and recipes, daily food plans, and a food tracker. It also contains lots of videos on a wide variety of topics related to nutrition.

Although I am not a medical professional or a nutritionist, I have consulted highly reputable sources to provide you with the key ingredients in your bipolar relapse prevention diet regimen. Note that certain conditions like hypertension (high blood pressure), high cholesterol, heart disease, and diabetes require specific dietary regimens, which you should develop and monitor in conjunction with your primary care physician, who should of course be informed of all your medications and that you have bipolar disorder. The recommendations in this book represent healthy behaviors that may help reduce the severity of your bipolar disorder.

GOOD NUTRITION

Eating healthy does not require a rigid diet, such as vegetarianism or eating only organic foods, but it does require a certain amount of discipline: you should eat only when you are hungry, eat on a regular schedule, and make considered food choices.

The first rule of good nutrition is to eat a lot of "whole foods," which means foods that are close to the way they occur in nature. The less your food is processed, the better, because processing reduces the nutritional benefits of food and also introduces higher levels of bad fats, sugar, and salt, which are not conducive to good health. In addition, processed and refined foods often have ingredients to which some people are sensitive or allergic. Therefore it is a good idea to minimize your intake of these foods.

The second rule of good nutrition is to look at where your calories are coming from. The general recommended number of calories for an adult is two thousand a day, but this varies according to weight, height, level of physical activity, and natural rate of metabolism. The Mayo Clinic (2013) recommends getting 45 to 65 percent of your daily caloric intake from carbohydrates and 10 to 35 percent from protein. We will look closely at these and certain other dietary components with a focus on their impact on your mood, brain functioning, and sleep—problems that can trigger bipolar relapse.

Carbohydrates

Carbohydrates are good for providing energy when you may be feeling depressed. A boost of energy may be just what you need to overcome the lethargy that often accompanies or precedes the sad feelings of depression.

Carbohydrates can be found naturally in plant-based foods and in particularly highly dense forms in legumes, fruits, milk, and whole grains. It is best to avoid the sugars found in sodas and desserts, as well as in grain products such as white flour (including baked goods made with white flour), white rice, and pasta—these grain products have been processed, meaning they've been bleached or bran and germ have been removed). A diet rich in brightly colored fruits and vegetables will ensure that you get the carbohydrates you need, as well as micronutrients such as vitamins A and D. The pale green iceberg lettuce in many salads and other dishes, for example, is not very high in nutrients. One way to get more carbohydrates in your diet is to substitute deep green leafy vegetables such as kale, chard, or spinach. Carrots—which, as you know, are bright orange—are another carbohydrate-rich vegetable. Melons, such as cantaloupes, and stone fruit, such as nectarines, also provide carbohydrates, with lots of vitamins as well.

Protein

Protein is important for human growth and development and helps adults maintain bone density, muscle composition, and healthy glucose (Layman 2009). It is also a source of long-term energy. There are both animal-based and plant-based sources of protein. Plant-based sources of protein, such as nuts, beans (including soy products), and lentils are most healthy. Meat, poultry, and dairy products are good sources of protein too, as long as they are lean or low in fat. It is a good idea to include some seafood in your diet—for example, two days a week. Because they contain omega-3 fatty acids (see below), shellfish and fish like salmon provide excellent support for brain function and are also a great source of protein.

Eating a good source of protein in the morning may help reduce your dependence on caffeine because it will both give you the energy you need to start the day and sustain you. Because it is a long-term energy source, protein helps your body maintain a stable level of energy that may also help stabilize your mood—by preventing, for example, the lack of energy that often precedes a full-blown episode of depression.

Fats

Fats help your brain function, keep your immune system working, and help your body absorb important nutrients. However, too much fat can be harmful, particularly trans fats and saturated fats, which can increase your bad cholesterol (low-density lipoprotein, or LDL) levels and your risk of heart disease. These fats, which are generally solid at room temperature (NIH 2011), include those in fatty meats, butter, and sausage, although butter (in moderation) is healthier than margarine. Butter is also healthier than some cooking oils that have hydrogenated oils. Hydrogenation, a process of adding hydrogen to food molecules, makes these oils thicker and more viscose but also harder for the body to process. Pure palm or corn oils are often hydrogenated to become cooking oils.

Your dietary emphasis should be on unsaturated fats, which are generally liquid at room temperature (NIH 2011). Unsaturated fats can lower your risk of heart disease and lower your levels of LDLs. Some good sources of unsaturated fats are fish, lean poultry, nuts, canola oil, peanut oil, corn oil, safflower oil, soy oil, cottonseed oil, vegetable oil, and olive oil. Even too much of these "healthy" fats, however, will increase your weight and put you at risk for obesity. Obesity creates other health problems, such as sleep apnea and physical discomfort, that can interfere with your sleep and put you at risk for bipolar relapse. (Though obesity is a particular concern for people with bipolar disorder because of bipolar medications that cause weight gain, this book will not focus on weight reduction strategies specifically, because any weight reduction program requires consultation with and supervision by a medical practitioner.)

Omega-3 fatty acids are an unsaturated fat. They're often found in cold-water fish, like salmon, mackerel, sardines, salmon, and herring; walnuts, canola, soybeans, and their oils; seeds such as flaxseed; extra-virgin olive oil; and fish oil supplements. Omega-3 fatty acids help keep your skin healthy and glowing, but more importantly, they help keep your brain functioning at its best. These polyunsaturated fats play a fundamental role in brain structure and function (especially docosahexaenoic acid, or DHA).

While some studies have found that omega-3 fatty acids have a negligible effect or no effect on mood disorders (Liperoti et al. 2009) or depression (Rogers et al. 2008; Stahl et al. 2008), other research suggests that omega-3 fatty acids might be an effective part of a comprehensive treatment plan for bipolar disorder. Omega-3 fatty acids have been found by Parker et al. (2006) and numerous other researchers to have a positive effect on mood in people with bipolar disorder, related mostly to their depressive symptoms (Chiu et al. 2005; Sarris, Mischoulon, and Schweitzer 2011). In other words, these fats may help elevate your mood. In another study, adolescents with juvenile bipolar disorder who were given omega-3 supplements for six weeks had significantly lower ratings of mania and depression, as well as lower ratings of problematic behaviors, and their overall functioning increased (Clayton et al. 2009).

Ultimately, although there are mixed findings regarding the impact of omega-3 fatty acids on functioning, a review of the evidence by a committee of the American Psychiatric Association found that use of omega-3 fatty acids for bipolar disorder is of potential benefit and negligible risk (Freeman et al. 2006). In other words, whether or not they help your bipolar disorder, increasing your intake of omega-3 fatty acids will not hurt. If you choose to take them in supplement form, a dose of 2 grams per day is recommended.

Do not confuse omega-3 fatty acids with omega-6 fatty acids, which are more common in most people's diets. Omega-6 fatty acids tend to contribute to inflammation in the body, while omega-3 fatty acids tend to reduce inflammation. Chronic inflammation can result in coronary disease, cancer, or other long-term illnesses. Soy oil, found in much of our snack food and processed foods, is probably the biggest source of omega-6 fatty acids. Reducing your consumption of processed foods will reduce your omega-6 levels.

Fiber

Fiber is important to people taking certain bipolar medications like lithium, which is a diuretic and often causes constipation. Vegetables and insoluble fibers such as wheat bran help reduce the risk of constipation. Reducing this uncomfortable and often painful side effect of medication may make you more willing to stick with your medication regimen, which in turn will reduce your likelihood of bipolar relapse. Soluble fiber, such as that found in some fruits (e.g., apples and oranges), oats, and beans helps your body process sugars. It also improves pancreas function and reduces your risk of diabetes. Avoiding chronic illnesses is key to staying healthy; furthermore, some medications for bipolar disorder, such as olanzapine, may increase your risk for diabetes, which can lead to renal disease. Thus keeping diabetes risk at a minimum is key to being able to maintain your medication regimen without causing damage to your organs.

Sodium

Heart disease, hypertension, and stroke are not medical conditions that you want to have to deal with in addition to your chronic illness of bipolar disorder. Limiting sodium (salt) in your diet reduces your risk of these other long-term problems. Foods that are high in sodium include processed foods (especially snacks such as chips), nuts, fast-food burgers and fries, and processed meats such as ham, salami, and other deli meats.

Sugar

As well as your intake of sodium, you should keep your intake of sugars to a minimum. The naturally occurring sugars found in most fruits and vegetables, some grains, and milk are much better than the refined sugars found in candy, desserts, and soda.

Water and Fluids

Because your body is 60 percent water by volume, drinking water is very important to keeping your body in good health. Eight glasses of water a day is what is generally recommended, but individual needs may differ. For this reason, try to pay attention to your body—frequent feelings of thirst or symptoms of thirst such as a dry mouth are the best indicators that you are not getting enough fluids. If drinking more plain water does not seem appealing, know that many fluids that contain water, such as juice, are also of benefit. Adding water, especially sparkling water, to juice can make increasing your water intake more exciting. My favorite is making fruit-flavored iced tea.

Staying hydrated will not only keep your kidneys functioning well, which is especially important if you are taking certain medications, but will keep you alert during the day, because dehydration makes you sleepy. A glass of water or other fluid can provide the same boost to your sleepy mind and body as a cup of caffeine. In fact, if you consume a lot of caffeinated drinks, then you may often be dehydrated, because caffeine is a diuretic. It also has a detrimental impact on your sleep, as was discussed in the previous chapter, so it may be best to avoid caffeine altogether if you are living with bipolar disorder.

Many bipolar medications, such as lithium, are diuretics, meaning that they take water out of your body. If you take any of these medications, you may notice that your mouth is dry and you need to urinate frequently; you may need to increase your fluid intake even further to avoid dehydration and to ameliorate side effects such as hand tremors.

Vitamin D

Vitamin D is an essential micronutrient that maintains healthy bone density and has a positive influence on mood. Vitamin D_3 is found in fatty fish, and because it is so important to our bodies it is added to many foods such as milk and some juices. Your body also produces vitamin D in response to sunlight, but nowadays dermatologists advise limiting your exposure to the sun's rays, and in the winter (when the days are shorter) natural light can be hard to come by. One of the side effects of taking antiepileptic drugs (e.g., lamotrigine or valproate) for bipolar disorder or other mental illness is a reduction of vitamin D in the blood (Ali et al. 2004), which can lead to osteoporosis. Consider increasing your intake of vitamin D or simply getting more sunlight— which may help you feel good whether science understands exactly how it works or not.

Tryptophan

The micronutrient L-tryptophan has been found to have a positive impact on mood, and a diet rich in tryptophan may be very helpful to people who are susceptible to depression (Sarris, Mischoulon, and Schweitzer 2011; Shabbir et al. 2013) because tryptophan appears to aid the transmission of serotonin (a biochemical) between neurons in the brain, and abnormalities in serotonin transmission have been linked to depression (Neumeister 2003). Foods that contain L-tryptophan include nuts, seeds, dates, eggs, meat, fish, tomatoes, and dairy products such as milk and cheese. As explained in chapter 3, tryptophan is a sleep inducer. This is why a glass of milk can help you sleep at night.

MONITORING AND TRACKING YOUR FOOD INTAKE

Tracking your food intake for at least one month will help you understand how the nutritional content of your diet influences the way you feel. Because of the complexity of tracking calories or nutritional content, and because there is so much variation in people's diets, there are no truly comprehensive tracking tools in this chapter. However, the resources listed at the end of this chapter can help you track fats, fiber, calories, carbohydrates, proteins, and other aspects of your diet. Several are free, and many are apps that you can download to your smartphone or computer.

Here is a daily log you can use to track your food intake, especially if you are making changes to your diet. It will help you see how your bipolar disorder is affected by these changes.

SAMPLE DAILY MOOD AND FOOD TRACKER

Date: 10/3/13

Time	Food	Mood Before	Mood After
7:30 a.m.	Coffee; pastry	Upbeat	Upbeat
Noon	Chicken sub; soda	Getting tired	Upbeat
3:00 p.m.	Doughnut & coffee	Sleepy	Wired
7:00 p.m.	Burrito and soda	Cranky and sleepy	Sleepy
10:00 p.m.	Cookies and milk	Bored	Unhappy

To use this Daily Mood and Food Tracker, every time you eat or drink, note the time. Then write down your mood or the reason you are eating or drinking. Sometimes you may eat for comfort or because you are bored, as shown in the example, so keeping track of why you are eating may help you understand not only what you eat, but why you eat. Eating healthy for bipolar disorder begins with knowing what you eat but also understanding why you eat and the impact it has on your mood.

This basic tracker will allow you to see what you eat on a daily basis and see how the foods you are eating may be influencing your mood. Use it for at least two weeks (preferably for one whole month, as mentioned) to help you notice any patterns in which your eating and your mood are related. Once you notice a pattern, you can try changing what and when you eat in order to change the way you feel.

If your mood is balanced and your diet is healthy and nutritious, you may want to keep track of your food intake just to see whether there are any patterns that show you what you are doing right. The Daily Mood and Food Tracker is also available on the publisher's website for this book (http://www.newharbinger.com/28814).

DAILY MOOD AND FOOD TRACKER

Date: _____

Time	Food	Mood Before	Mood After

NUTRITION AND BIPOLAR MEDICATIONS

Keeping your medication regimen stable will help keep your mood stable, but a poor diet might lead to situations in which a change in medication is needed. For example, a diet that puts you at high risk for diabetes may affect your mental health care provider's decision to prescribe olanzapine because it can also increase your risk of diabetes. Sometimes medication changes cannot be helped, but there is no point in precipitating them through an unhealthy diet. Changing medications requires significant patience and monitoring effort, and new combinations often result in new side effects, which may cause you unnecessary stress.

Because medications interact with various biochemical and metabolic processes in your body, it is best to have a nutritional routine that is also stable. Think of the nutrients that you put in your body as medications for your body: keeping the system stable helps keep your mood stable. Binge eating, binge drinking, or drastically changing your eating patterns can affect how your body reacts to the medications that you are taking.

The Impact of Side Effects

All medications may have side effects. The key to success in treating any condition such as bipolar disorder is finding the right medication for you, one with a minimum of side effects and maximum benefit to your mental health. Some drugs may not cause you any side effects, but learning to manage side effects has a strong influence on whether or not you adhere to your medication regimen.

There is not enough room for me to discuss all the medications for bipolar disorder, but many have similar side effects. Lithium (a mood stabilizer) may put your kidneys and liver at risk, so regular monitoring of kidney functioning (with checkups usually every three months) is essential to good health in people who take such medications. As stated above, lots of water and other fluids will help your body counteract the diuretic effects of lithium. Other medications, such as olanzapine (an antipsychotic), will affect your pancreatic functioning and thus increase your risk of diabetes. If you are on such medications, then a discussion with your doctor about ways to change your diet to lower your intake of sugars is important to maintain proper metabolic functioning and not add another chronic condition to your existing bipolar disorder.

Sometimes medications like olanzapine, whose possible side effects also include increased appetite and weight gain, may only be needed at times when your bipolar symptoms are not being controlled by other medications. In such cases, your exposure to these side effects may only be for a short time.

Remember to take all medications as prescribed and report any side effects to your health care providers so that they can help find the medication or combination of medications that works best for you.

The Effect of Grapefruit and Citrus Juices on Bipolar Medications

Although citrus fruit and juices, especially grapefruit juice, are good sources of vitamin C and other nutrients, they are known to interact with certain medications. Grapefruit juice is known to affect the uptake (the rate of absorption) of certain substances and the bioavailability (how much is available to the body) of others, and thus it is specifically contraindicated for some medications. These include several medications for bipolar disorder, such as olanzapine. Eating grapefruits or drinking grapefruit juice while you are on olanzapine will affect the way your body processes the active ingredient in the medication.

Interaction with grapefruit juice has been studied for forty different drugs (Saito et al. 2005). Because of the complexity involved in measuring intake and the magnitude of interactions, it is challenging to predict the extent of grapefruit product–drug interactions (Seden et al. 2010). Therefore, people taking medications for mental illness should avoid grapefruits and grapefruit juice until the psychological community can give firm recommendations. Read the warnings that come with your medication, and discuss with your mental health care provider any risk of citrus/grapefruit interactions with any medications you are taking.

Note: For people with bipolar disorder who have to take hormone substitutes such as levothyroxine, it appears that although there is some effect of grapefruit juice on absorption of the hormone, it does not affect the availability of the hormone to the endocrine system (Lilja, Laitinen, and Neuvonen 2005).

BIPOLAR DISORDER AND WEIGHT

Because bipolar disorder leads to depression, it carries a risk of obesity due to overeating related to depression. Although the impact of medications and the occurrence of side effects vary from one person to another, many medications that treat the symptoms of bipolar disorder also put people with bipolar disorder at risk of gaining weight, either through increased appetite or through interference with metabolism. This can then lead to poor mental and physical health (Wildes, Marcus, and Fagiolini 2006). One study of veterans found that those with bipolar disorder were more likely to have poor exercise and eating habits than those without bipolar disorder (Kilbourne et al. 2007). Anyone with bipolar disorder knows how easy it is to slip into bad habits when she or he is struggling to keep sane.

According to Mayo Clinic psychiatrist Daniel Hall-Flavin (2012), some of the other drugs used to treat bipolar disorder that cause weight gain are divalproex sodium (Depakote), carbamazepine (Tegretol), and lamotrigine (Lamictal). Some antipsychotics, such as risperidone (Risperdal), quetiapine (Seroquel), and aripiprazole (Abilify), also cause weight gain. Hall-Flavin also states that weight gain appears more likely when an antipsychotic is combined with a mood stabilizer, which is a common combination in medication protocols for bipolar disorder. With regard to antidepressants, Hall-Flavin states that weight gain is more likely with older drugs, such as tricyclic antidepressants and some monoamine oxidase inhibitors (MAOIs).

When you find yourself tempted to eat more than usual for whatever reason, it is best to find low-calorie options to satisfy your appetite. For example, grapes and carrots make great snack alternatives to potato chips or candy, and they are very low in calories and high in nutrients, with antioxidants to give your body's immune system more fighting power.

If you are already overweight and want to monitor your diet to lose weight, it is best to combine your dietary changes with exercise. No matter what you decide to do, you should visit your primary health care provider to discuss how changes in your diet and exercise routine may affect your mental and physical health.

CAFFEINE, ALCOHOL, NICOTINE, AND BIPOLAR DISORDER

All three of these substances have negative impacts on the mental well-being of people with bipolar disorder because of their influence on mood. Caffeine (found in chocolate, coffee, and some teas such as green and black teas) and alcohol have been shown to influence mood (Childs and de Wit 2006; Gonzalez-Bono et al. 2002; Goldstein, Velyvis, and Parikh 2006; Parker, Parker, and Brotchie 2006). Nicotine dependence has also been found to be related to increase in risk of depression (Grover, Goodwin, and Zvolensky 2012). These substances influence brain chemistry in ways that may trigger a mood episode. As mentioned in chapter 3, they interfere with sleep. They may also interact negatively with any medications you may be taking. That does not mean that you can never have caffeine, alcohol, or nicotine again, but you should have them in moderation and monitor your intake using the Weekly Triggers and Mood chart in chapter 2 so that you can see what effect, if any, they have on your bipolar symptoms. Moderating or eliminating all three will allow your medications to work as they should, keep your mood more stable (no "down" from alcohol or "up" from nicotine and caffeine), and give you a better night's sleep. Everyone is different, and alcohol, nicotine, or coffee may influence different people's moods in different ways. That is why monitoring their impact on you is important for understanding your triggers for mood episodes.

Alcohol

Alcohol is a mood-altering substance that some people with bipolar disorder may use to "self-medicate," either to drown their emotions or to calm mania. Alcohol also interacts with many medications for bipolar disorder. The container for these medications will feature a warning label not to use alcohol while taking them. So a good rule when it comes to alcohol is to have none at all or to have only one drink (one glass of wine, one ounce of spirits, or one twelve-ounce can or bottle of beer) in any given day. Any use of alcohol in conjunction with your prescription medications is something you should discuss with your medical provider because of the possibility for negative interactions.

Substance abuse is very common among people with bipolar disorder (National Institute of Mental Health n.d.). To assess whether you may have a problem with alcohol use and abuse, you can use the following set of questions (adapted from Ewing 1984). Answering yes to any two questions indicates that you should explore your use of alcohol and its impact on your life with your primary care provider, your mental health care provider, or a substance abuse counselor. This person will help you understand whether alcohol is getting in the way of your mental health and sabotaging your efforts to stabilize your mood and avoid manic or depressive episodes. Getting help with any misuse of alcohol will go a long way toward reducing the frequency and intensity of any bipolar symptoms that you are experiencing. Here are the questions:

1. Do you feel you drink too much?

2. Are you bothered by people who criticize you about your drinking?

3. Does your drinking make you feel guilty?

4. Do you need a drink to start the day to deal with a hangover?

Caffeine

Because caffeine is an ingredient in so many different products, it is important to account for your overall intake in order to assess how it is impacting your mood, sleep, and overall quality of life. I have provided the following chart (adapted from White and Preston 2009) to help you assess your daily intake of caffeine.

	Amount of Caffeine	Quantity per Day	Total mg per Day
Beverages/Chocolate			
Coffee (6 oz)	125 mg	× _____	= _____
Decaf coffee (6 oz)	5 mg	× _____	= _____
Espresso (1 oz)	50 mg	× _____	= _____
Tea (6 oz)	50 mg	× _____	= _____
Green tea (6 oz)	20 mg	× _____	= _____
Hot cocoa (6 oz)	15 mg	× _____	= _____
Caffeinated soft drinks (12 oz)	40–60 mg	× _____	= _____
Chocolate candy bar (100 g)	20 mg	× _____	= _____
Over-the-Counter Medications			
Anacin	32 mg/pill	× _____	= _____
Appetite-control pills	100–200 mg/ pill	× _____	= _____
Dristan	16 mg/pill	× _____	= _____
Excedrin	65 mg/pill	× _____	= _____
Extra Strength Excedrin	100 mg/pill	× _____	= _____
Midol	132 mg/pill	× _____	= _____
NoDoz	100 mg/pill	× _____	= _____
Triaminicin	30 mg/pill	× _____	= _____
Vanquish	33 mg/pill	× _____	= _____
Vivarin	200 mg/pill	× _____	= _____
Prescription Medications			
Cafergot	100 mg/pill	× _____	= _____
Fiorinal	40 mg/pill	× _____	= _____
Darvon compound	32 mg/pill	× _____	= _____
Total mg Caffeine per Day			_____

The recommended daily intake of caffeine is no more than 250 mg, so as not to interfere with sleep (Barone and Roberts 1996). As you know if you have read chapter 3, a healthy sleep pattern is a very important way to minimize mood episodes. Therefore, limiting your caffeine intake is very important to your overall mental health. If you find that your caffeine intake is above 250 mg, then you will want to cut back. As mentioned in chapter 3, you may also want to restrict your caffeine to the early part of the day (e.g., before noon) so that your body will have plenty of time to process it before your bedtime.

TIPS FOR HEALTHY EATING

The following tips for healthy eating come from the US Department of Agriculture's Center for Nutrition Policy and Promotion (2011):

1. *Balance calories.* Include a wide variety of foods in your diet, with an emphasis on proteins and complex carbohydrates rather than fats and sugars.

2. *Enjoy your food but eat less.* Focus on your feelings of hunger to know when you should eat and on your feelings of fullness to know when you should stop eating.

3. *Avoid oversized portions.* Use smaller plates and bowls. When you are ordering at a restaurant, ask the server about portion sizes, to help you decide what you want to eat. A good trick is to ask for half your meal in a take-away container and eat only half your meal at the table. Skimp on desserts, which can sometimes seem like an entire meal.

4. *Eat more fruits, vegetables, and whole grains.* They contain fiber and essential nutrients such as calcium, vitamin D, and potassium.

5. *Make half your plate fruits and vegetables*, especially red, dark green, and orange vegetables. Choose a salad as a side dish instead of french fries or mashed potatoes. A fruit salad at

breakfast or a green salad at dinner makes an excellent appe-
tizer or side dish. Fruit is also a great choice for dessert.

6. *Switch to low-fat dairy products* such as low-fat yogurt, low-fat
   milk, and low-fat cheeses.

7. *Make at least half your grains whole grains.* Choose whole-grain
   cereals, breads, and snacks, and choose brown rice instead of
   white rice.

8. *Minimize your intake of solid fats, added sugars, and salt.* This
   includes popular foods like pizza, cookies, cakes, sausage,
   bacon, sodas, and ice cream. Sprinkle these in your diet as
   "treats" instead of eating them every day.

9. *Compare sodium in foods*, especially in processed foods like
   canned soups, chips, processed meats, and frozen foods. Buy
   reduced-sodium varieties of these foods if you can—or, better
   yet, eat fresh.

10. *Drink water instead of sugary drinks.* Many fortified drinks
    include high levels of sugar. If you drink sports drinks for their
    vitamins or electrolytes, you may want to dilute them with
    water to reduce the amount of sugar you take in. You can use
    juices to flavor your water by adding one part juice to two parts
    water. You can also flavor your water with a slice of lime,
    lemon, orange, or cucumber; a piece of ginger; or a mint leaf.
    Another options is to drink your water in the form of iced tea,
    making sure that it's non-caffeinated.

For more details of these tips, see "10 Tips to a Great Plate" at
http://www.choosemyplate.gov/food-groups/downloads/TenTips
/DGTipsheet1ChooseMyPlate-BlkAndWht.pdf.

CHALLENGES TO HEALTHY EATING

Sometimes the best intentions get waylaid by the challenges of life.
Simply being away from home often presents a challenge to sticking

with the kind of diet that promotes health and mental well-being and helps prevent bipolar relapse. The major threats to good nutrition are time constraints, restaurants, friends and family, travel, and special events.

Time Constraints

Time constraints can sabotage your efforts to maintain a diet that does not put your health at risk because fast foods contain high amounts of salt, sugar, and processed foods. The best way to meet the challenge that time constraints pose to healthy eating is to be prepared with food that you have brought from home. Bring your own lunch to work. Carry snacks that require little or no prep time like baby carrots, oranges, celery, grapes, and sliced fruit. Make sure to eat breakfast at home and you will be less hungry throughout the day. If you must have a quick bite while you are out, eat fresh as much as you can, because whole foods are good for you and contain the nutrients you need to keep going without the bad stuff that will get in the way of your nutritional objectives.

Restaurants

Restaurants are a challenge to healthy eating because when you eat out, you are not in control of portion size. The offerings also tend to be higher in fat and salt than you may want for your new healthy self. To meet this challenge, first, as mentioned, ask your server about the size of the portions or look around you at what other people are eating before you order. If the servings are large, then ask for half of your order to be served to you in the restaurant and the other half to take home for lunch or dinner the next day. Order foods that have not been cooked for a long time (the less cooked it is, the more nutrients it contains), vegetables and fruits that are bright in color, and foods that are low in fat and salt. Many restaurants have diabetic and heart-friendly options or offer special meals for people with restricted diets, such as diabetics, vegetarians, or people with hypertension. Ask your server about these meals, which may not be featured on the menu. They will provide you with the carbohydrates and nutrient-rich vegetables that promote good health while also limiting your sugar and salt.

Friends and Family

Your friends and family can be a challenge to healthy eating if they are not as concerned with healthy eating as you are. Spending time with your friends and family and going to social gatherings may include having to resist the strong lure of foods you are trying to avoid. People may encourage you to set aside your healthy eating patterns. As will be discussed in the chapter on people (chapter 6), it may help to tell the people you often spend time with that you are trying to eat healthy so that you can be healthier in mind and body. Social support for your efforts may be what you need to keep you from succumbing to the temptations of unhealthy eating patterns.

For many people, a night on the town with friends may involve drinking alcohol and taking non-prescribed drugs. If you are focused on preventing bipolar relapse, you need to limit (or eliminate) your intake of alcohol and non-prescribed medications when you go out.

Travel

Travel is a challenge to healthy eating because when you are traveling, you are not in control of portion size and you may not always know the nutritional value of what it is that you are eating. Like restaurants, many airlines offer special meals for people with restricted diets, but you will need to ask about these. If you are traveling abroad, when dining at a restaurant you will have to ask the server more questions. If this requires fluency in a foreign language, you may want to find someone to translate for you. Or better yet, memorize how to ask important questions related to your preferences before you leave home.

If you have a restricted diet for diabetes or are vegan or vegetarian, you may face even greater challenges to eating healthy when you travel. A great option that may also help you explore your surroundings is to ask for the nearest market and buy yourself fresh foods. Try new things and learn how to eat or prepare them. You may add a few items to your list of foods to choose from. But just in case, bring along some protein-dense snacks (like protein bars), to sustain you if you cannot find suitable options on the road.

Special Events

Celebrations, meetings, and holidays can present a special challenge to your eating program because you are in the company of people who are using food to enjoy a special event together. Eating can be a way of bonding and of sharing a particular experience, and the temptation to go beyond your limits can be difficult to resist. In this case, don't deny yourself the experience outright; enjoy the different foods that are available, but do so moderately. Limit your portions of the least healthy foods or those foods that you know will trigger your bipolar symptoms (e.g., highly processed foods, alcohol, or caffeine—look back over your Daily Mood and Food Tracker) while eating as much as you can of the healthier foods. If you start by eating your fill of foods that give you good nutrition and are not a trigger for your bipolar symptoms, then you won't have room for foods that present more of a problem for your physical and mental health and well-being.

A MEAL PLAN

Preparing for change and having a structure for change helps support efforts for change. Be proactive in deciding what you will eat by filling out a simple meal plan. See the following example.

SAMPLE WEEKLY MEAL PLAN

Food & Drink	Mon. 12/5	Tues. 12/6	Wed. 12/7	Thur. 12/8	Fri. 12/9	Sat. 12/10	Sun. 12/11
Breakfast	Oatmeal with banana	Yogurt	Scrambled eggs	Oatmeal with berries	Cereal with milk	Yogurt with berries	Muffin, Coffee
Snack	Orange	Fruit smoothie	Popcorn	Orange	Apple	Nuts	Cheese
Lunch	Chicken salad sandwich	Veggie soup with bread	Pasta with veggies	Pizza	Salad	Tacos	Brunch buffet
Snack	Carrots	Apple	Grapes	Cookies	Yogurt	Cereal bar	Pastry
Dinner	Grilled chicken & salad	Veggie stir fry with shrimp and noodles	Lasagna	Chicken salad	Omelet with salmon	Sushi	Steak with vegetables and mashed potatoes

Consider the information in your Mood and Food Tracker when developing your meal plan. You may also want to confer with your medical provider and a nutritionist (if you can afford one).

Preparing these foods at home will make it more likely that you will stick to your menu. It also will go a long way toward keeping more money in your pocket, because prepared foods cost more. You can photocopy the following chart, create your own version, or download one from the publisher's website for this book at http://www.newhar binger.com/28814.

WEEKLY MEAL PLAN

Food & Drink	Mon.	Tues.	Wed.	Thur.	Fri.	Sat.	Sun.
Breakfast							
Snack							
Lunch							
Snack							
Dinner							

RESOURCES

For those who like to cook, Epicurious is a free iPhone app that helps you plan meals (it contains thousands of recipes) and make shopping lists. There are also many other apps available to help you track your nutrition and diet, as well as the following online logs and diaries.

- Inspiring Nutrition's "Food Diary" (http://www.personal -nutrition-guide.com/support-files/free_food_diary.pdf)

  This is a simple, straightforward log that includes one page per day, with lots of room for recording the various times you ate during the day. You track time and what you ate or drank, the amount, and calories. There is a blank column, which could be used for mood.

- MyFoodDiary (http://www.myfooddiary.com)

  A much more comprehensive diary, MyFoodDiary is an online calorie counter with diet journal and exercise log. You have to pay for all the extras, but there is a free trial. The site offers an iPhone app and the ability to graph your information so that you can track your progress visually.

- US Department of Agriculture's "SuperTracker" (https://www.supertracker.usda.gov/default.aspx)

  SuperTracker allows you to compare the nutrition values of over eight thousand foods. Using a food tracker, weight manager, and physical activity tracker, you can develop a personalized nutrition and physical activity plan. There is also a goal tracker and a recipe section that allows you to save your favorite recipes.

For More Information

An excellent resource on nutrition on the web is ChooseMyPlate .gov (http://www.choosemyplate.gov), which is sponsored by the US Department of Agriculture. It is bright, colorful, and easy to read and navigate, and you can use it to order or download dozens of free resources on all components of a healthy diet. There are trackers, food plans, calorie counters, and other tools for keeping your diet healthy, and thus reducing your risk of bipolar relapse. The "10 Tips Nutrition Education" series offers tips on many aspects of eating healthy, including focusing on fruits and vegetables, making good choices when shopping for food, making good beverage choices, and healthy nutrition for children.

SUMMARY

Eating for mental health means eating a healthy, nutrient-rich diet that feeds your body and your mind. Making sure that you eat a balanced diet of carbohydrates, protein, fats, and fiber will help your body function at its best, which will support your mental health and help prevent bipolar relapse. Buying healthy foods and filling your cupboards with them will help limit your access to foods that do not benefit your body or may trigger your bipolar symptoms.

CHAPTER 5

ACTIVITY

As part of the SNAP approach to preventing bipolar relapse, "activity" means more than just physical activity—it includes any kind of recreational activity that keeps your interest, feeds your passions, and makes you happy. Pleasant or relaxing distractions such as fishing, knitting, or reading may help keep your mood stable and your stress levels low. However, the focus of this chapter will be on physical activity, because that is the form of activity that most research in this area has focused on. In other words, other kinds of activity, though they may be beneficial, have not yet been shown to be as effective at helping prevent bipolar relapse as moving your body.

If you are like many people with bipolar disorder, you may not be getting enough physical activity. A study (Kilbourne et al. 2007) found that people with bipolar disorder were more likely than people without a diagnosis of serious mental illness to report poor exercise habits, including infrequent walking or strength exercises, and were also more likely to report poor eating habits. They were also more likely to have gained weight in the past month. In fact, there is a strong link between weight gain and bipolar disorder (Keck and McElroy 2006).

When you think of physical activity, you may think of an exercise regimen that requires discipline, specialized equipment, a gym membership, and perhaps a personal trainer. However, physical activity encompasses much more. Exercise as most people think of it—such as walking, running, and swimming, all simply for the sake of exercise—is part of a physically active lifestyle, but there are many other ways to stay moving that contribute to a healthy body and a healthy mind. Later in this chapter, I will list some strategies for getting more physical activity in ways that do.not necessarily involve working up a sweat.

Note: Before you start any exercise program, it is important that you consult with your medical provider so that you do not put your health at risk.

THE GENERAL BENEFITS OF EXERCISE

It is clear that the body was meant to move. Regular physical activity has multiple long-term benefits for everyone, regardless of their mental or physical state. For example, it helps maintain a healthy weight, improves heart and lung function, and strengthens the immune system. It also combats health conditions and diseases. According to Harvard Medical School (2013), "Exercise is the best kept secret in preventive medicine," and regular exercise can protect against heart attack, stroke, high blood pressure, diabetes, obesity, dementia, and breast and colon cancers.

Rather than focus on the long-term benefits, however, people should focus on the short-term benefits as reason to exercise (Stevens and Bryan 2012). According to research, exercise induces chemical changes in the brain that improve brain functioning, decrease depressive symptoms, and increase overall mental well-being (Williams and Strean 2006). Regular exercise can help improve low mood and ameliorates the symptoms of anxiety, stress, and depressive disorders (Otto and Smits 2011). According to the Mayo Clinic (2011), regular physical activity can also be fun, promote better sleep, give you more energy, and put the spark back into your sex life. Thus exercise can improve your overall quality of life in short order.

Although the long-term health benefits of exercise are important and not to be trivialized in any way, your focus should be on preventing bipolar relapse using physical activity to improve your mood. The future reduction in the risk of heart disease, stroke, and diabetes, as well as the overall feeling of healthiness that comes with regular physical activity, is the bonus to doing the work that will keep you from experiencing symptoms of bipolar disorder.

THE BENEFITS OF EXERCISE FOR BIPOLAR DISORDER

The evidence is clear that exercise is good for people who are living with bipolar disorder. A study of adolescents with bipolar disorder showed that eight weeks of aerobic exercise had a significant positive impact on depressive moods and mania (Piri et al. 2012). And a review of eight studies that used physical exercise as an intervention to treat major depression showed that the subjects' mood improved in seven of those studies and that regardless of the mechanism of action (which is not clearly understood), the mood-enhancing effect of exercise is irrefutable (Eriksson and Gard 2011).

People with mood disorders such as bipolar disorder are at increased risk for type 2 diabetes (Poulin et al. 2005), and some atypical antipsychotics such as olanzapine (commonly prescribed for bipolar disorder) increase risk for diabetes and weight gain. Weight gain is a significant issue, because it is a common side effect of certain medications for bipolar disorder, and many people with bipolar disorder find that it makes taking these medications problematic; thus the side effect of weight gain contributes to non-adherence to medication protocols meant to prevent bipolar relapse. Physical activity can help stave off both diabetes and weight gain—whether they are related to your bipolar disorder itself, to your medications for it, or to other factors.

However, the emotional ups and downs of bipolar disorder, which often lead to inconsistent physical activity and treatment (both medication and psychotherapy) adherence, may interfere with your best intentions to keep on track with a physical activity program. You may also face many other obstacles to your fitness regimen. But, as you will see, there are ways to deal with just about all of them.

OVERCOMING CHALLENGES TO PHYSICAL ACTIVITY

People give lots of reasons for not leading a physically active lifestyle. Some are based on their perceptions of what it takes to be physically active, and others are based on their circumstances. Below is a list of some of the most common reasons people (including me) give for not taking the time to treat their mind and bodies to some physical activity, even when they know that it can help them live longer, happier, healthier lives and prevent the symptoms of bipolar disorder.

- Lack of time

- Lack of energy

- Lack of enjoyment

- Lack of money

- Lack of child care

- Lack of company

- Lack of success

- Bipolar symptoms

I will present some solutions to each of these "problems." If your problem is a lack of ideas of what to do, the section "Choosing Your Activity" later in this chapter should prove helpful.

LACK OF TIME

"I don't have time" is probably the most popular excuse for not doing physical activity. However, physical activity helps you sleep better, which makes you more alert during the day, which makes you more efficient at work and other tasks. When you think about it in that way, physical activity actually adds more time to your day. So consider physical activity a way of making your day longer while improving your mood.

The things we do reflect our priorities. There are lots of ways to fit the exercise you need into your day to show that one of your priorities is exercising to stay healthy. One way is to make it the first thing you do every day. Getting up an hour earlier than usual to exercise (which means going to bed an hour earlier) will make sure you start the day in a good mood and with one thing on your bipolar relapse prevention "checklist" already done. You could also use your lunchtime to exercise, leaving enough time to eat after you do. Exercising at lunchtime is a good way to ensure that you do not work through lunch, eat at your desk, or eat a heavy, unhealthy lunch. Plus, the resulting increase in metabolism will help your body use the nutrients you take in when you are done exercising. At home, perhaps you can get your family members to help with or take over chores that you normally do so that you have more time for physical activity. Or you might hire a housekeeper or have your clothes washed and folded at a laundry as a way of getting household chores out of your way. You could even hire someone to prepare meals at your home several times per week if you can afford it.

If you have a desk job, or if you use a desk at home, you might also consider asking your employer for a desk that allows you to stand, or buying yourself one. Because it takes more energy to stand than sit while working, this is one small way to increase your level of activity that does not require any time at all.

The "Strategies for Increasing Your Activity Level Even Further" at the end of this chapter can help you squeeze even more physical activity into your day. For example, you can park at the far end of your office parking lot so that you are forced to walk a little extra distance. Better yet, if it is not too far, ride a bicycle or walk to work. Use the stairs instead of the elevator, visit your coworkers in person instead of e-mailing or calling them, or hand deliver documents to other offices at your location instead of sending them through interoffice mail. At the very least, you can take periodic breaks at work to take a short walk, climb the stairs, or do some simple exercises. Giving your mind a break from work in this way will reduce your stress and increase your mental effectiveness, so it is good for you all around.

LACK OF ENERGY

"I don't have energy" is another common reason for not exercising. But just as physical activity creates time, it also creates energy. Physical activity gets your adrenaline going, increases your metabolism, and gives you energy throughout the day, especially if you are getting the nutrients you need for healthy living. If you lack energy it may be due to stress, poor nutrition (see chapter 4), or sleep problems (see chapter 3) or because symptoms of mania or depression are interfering with the amount and quality of your sleep. "Forcing" yourself to get exercise when you have no energy is one way to get more energy and to stave off or alleviate an episode of depression. When you are feeling symptoms or triggers of depression, physical activity may seem like a tremendous challenge, but it is well worth it because of the significant benefits to be had at a time when you may be experiencing the early onset of a mood episode or be at risk of having one.

LACK OF ENJOYMENT

People who say "I don't like to exercise" often consider physical activity something you do in a gym with a group of people or with lots of high-end equipment, but, as mentioned, there are many other ways to increase the level of physical activity in your life.

I like to think of exercise as "medication" that helps treat the symptoms of bipolar disorder. And the great thing about this "medication" is that it has many positive side effects but very few negative ones. Being in great health is something we would all like, and if you think of exercise as part of having a healthy life, then you may find yourself liking exercise because you like what it brings you: better mental functioning, better physical health, and an overall feeling of well-being.

Much of the time when people say they do not like to exercise it is because they are thinking of specific types of physical activities that they do not enjoy. As I said earlier, having an active lifestyle is not necessarily about exercise per se but about keeping your body moving. There are many ways to move, and finding one that suits your preference and lifestyle will help you start and maintain a routine.

Walking, especially on nice days or with someone you love, can be very enjoyable even for the least athletically inclined among us. You may choose to keep a comfortable pair of shoes in your car so that you can go for a walk any time you want, anywhere you want. You may choose to go on a walking date with a friend or partner instead of sitting and eating or sitting and watching a movie. You may choose to explore meditative ways of moving that relax your mind while strengthening and relaxing your body, such as tai chi or yoga. Martial arts such as karate and tae kwon do not only improve your mental focus, physical strength, and flexibility, but also have built-in incentives: different color belts as you progress in knowledge and ability. You may love the camaraderie of fitness classes such as Zumba (if you love to dance), spinning (if you love to cycle), or boxing or kickboxing (if you like a more aggressive and physical form of activity). Depending on where you live, hiking and kayaking may be pleasurable options that take you into nature, which has a calming effect on the psyche. Or joining a fundraising exercise group (for example, for breast cancer) may provide you with the social support you need to meet your physical activity goals and a potential source of friends.

LACK OF MONEY

If you say, "I don't have the money," you probably have the perception that all physical activity takes place in a room with other people who have also paid to be there. The cost of group exercise, whether it be a yoga class, a spinning class, an aqua fitness class, or a strength and conditioning class, can be prohibitive. But there are lots of free or inexpensive ways to get the physical activity that will keep your mind and body healthy.

The first of these is walking, which is a very efficient and effective way to keep your body moving. You may be surprised to learn that for many fitness experts, an "active lifestyle" requires nothing more than walking a total of ten thousand steps (about six miles or 10k) a day. This can include the walking you do to and from your car, while on a hike, or while shopping in a mall. This is a lot of walking, but you can do it if you make it a goal. Note that there is no "failure" in not getting exactly that many steps each day, but it gives you something to work toward. Walking requires a minimal investment in a comfortable pair of walking shoes and comfortable clothes. With the right shoes, it may simply mean a change of shoes after work. No special clothes are required; neither are there any monthly fees or even parking costs (depending on where you go for a walk).

If walking is not your thing, you can use a home fitness program that follows a book or DVD, perhaps from your local library. You can play a video game that requires physical activity (e.g., a fitness, sports, or dancing game for any popular modern console with a motion controller), or you can exercise along with videos on YouTube (http://www.youtube.com). Community centers, colleges, and universities sometimes offer free or low-cost classes in physical education, and your local gym may offer discounts or free classes as an incentive to join. Free classes may give you some ideas to help you design your exercise program, so take advantage of these.

Doing calisthenic or walking exercises or running on a home treadmill, elliptical, or stationary bicycle may require an initial investment, but if you do it while watching television you may get a high return on your investment. You may also find that you invest less in workout clothes if you are exercising at home. You can find exercise equipment online at deeply discounted prices and also at thrift stores.

If none of these options appeal to you, you may want to consider the cost of going swimming (a good activity for people with injuries, arthritis, or any other physical challenges that may restrict their ability to walk or run), taking yoga classes (which are great for keeping your mood stable), or hiring a personal trainer as an investment in your mental and physical health. Given the price of cocktails and fancy coffee drinks, you may find that the money you save by reducing or eliminating alcohol and caffeine from your diet (not to mention quitting smoking) as recommended in chapter 4 is enough to help you compound the positive effect on your health by covering the expenses of an exercise program.

You can save a lot of money on workout gear, exercise equipment, and sporting goods by buying used. Visit a thrift store or any shop that sells used fitness equipment. Personally, I have found swim goggles at a tiny fraction of their original cost, tennis rackets, and even a set of weights, each for less than $10, at my neighborhood thrift stores. You may also find free or cheap used equipment on Craigslist (http://www .craigslist.org) or by using the Freecycle Network (http://www.free cycle.org).

Lastly, you may choose to join a fundraising exercise program that provides free coaching in exchange for raising money for a particular charity like lymphoma or breast cancer. You will have not only the company of other people focused on a charitable goal, but also the benefit of good coaching and the accomplishment of a significant physical activity goal at the end. This can be highly motivating, because you can see your progress, feel proud of reaching your goal, and become more aware of what your body can do.

LACK OF CHILD CARE

Lack of child care is a very valid reason for not doing physical activity, but this assumes that physical activity must take place outside the home. As I pointed out in the previous section, you can do many kinds of physical activity without leaving home—such as walking in place (e.g., while watching television), calisthenics, yoga, Wii Fit, or any computer- or television-based fitness program.

If you have an infant or toddler, carrying your child (for example, in a sling) as you go about your chores will keep him or her content and also make your chores more of a workout. If you carry your young child when you go for a walk, you will burn more calories and increase your cardiovascular fitness and muscle strength. It is even more efficient if you bring your dog along (if you have one). I have seen some highly motivated mothers with two young children in a stroller and a dog on a leash while they go for a run. At the very least, it is a way for everyone to get some fresh air and can reduce the isolation that often comes from being at home with young children. Older children can join you for a walk and the whole family gets the benefit of your new physical activity program. (Your child will also get better sleep as a result.) Weather may pose a challenge to getting outside, but if you dress appropriately and do the same for your children, the good feelings of being outside may compensate for any inconvenience from the weather.

Child care expenses can really add to the cost of a physical activity program. If the program you choose to follow puts you in need of child care to facilitate your goals, one way to save money is to trade child care with someone else who wants to exercise but also needs child care. For example, you watch the children on Monday, Wednesday, and Friday, and the other person watches the children on Tuesday, Thursday, and Saturday—this way you both get three days a week of physical activity.

If your child is involved in a sport or other extracurricular activity, make the most of that time to increase your own level of physical activity. For example, if you must wait for your children while they play soccer or learn to swim, instead of sitting in the stands reading a magazine or playing a game on your electronic device, you can walk around the outside of the soccer field, use the free lane in the pool, or schedule another physical activity for these times.

Parents' groups and community centers often offer parent-child exercise programs. These programs allow you to have fun bonding with your child while getting your physical activity needs met and meeting other mothers or fathers who may become members of your social support network (see chapter 6).

Equipment built for two, like a tandem kayak or bicycle, and accommodations like a bicycle trailer or child carrier can allow you to participate with your young children in a physical activity that can become a family tradition. When my daughter was a toddler, I used to carry her on my back as I went hiking. I would take a break and we would picnic, and then she would hike for as long as she could, and when she got tired I would put her back in the carrier. I have also gone kayaking with my daughter since she was quite young, and it is an activity we still enjoy doing together. Taking your child along with you when you do physical activity sets a positive example. I believe, for example, that our activities together helped instill in my daughter a lifelong love for the outdoors. Other activities that you can do with your child include bicycle riding (on separate bikes), roller blading or skating, ice skating, tennis, skiing, or even running, depending on your child's age and level of physical ability.

LACK OF COMPANY

Finding an "exercise buddy" to pair up with can increase your accountability and enhance your performance because it gives you someone to support you as you push yourself to achieve your physical activity goals. If you have children, perhaps you can include them in your physical activity somehow, as discussed in the previous section. Or talk to your friends or people from your gym (or wherever you exercise) and find someone with whom you can carpool or with whom you can take a walk. It does not have to be the same person all the time; you could have someone you walk with on Mondays and Wednesdays and someone else you walk with on Tuesdays and Thursdays. Meetup (http://www.meetup.org), Craigslist (http://www .craigslist.org), parents' groups, community centers, community boards, hiking clubs, and e-mail lists are all good resources for finding people with whom you can be active in a way that suits you. You are not the only one who wants support in maintaining an active lifestyle! You may join interest groups to have a variety of activities to choose from so that you do not get bored and also as a way to make friends. If you have the money to hire one, a personal trainer will ensure that you always have company, support, and motivation to implement a physical activity plan that is tailored for you.

LACK OF SUCCESS

Because physical activity, in conjunction with a change in diet, is often part of a weight-loss effort, people who have previously failed to lose weight (or keep off the weight they initially lost) when they increased their physical activity may think that exercise simply does not work for them. Remember that increasing your physical activity is primarily about your *mental* health; once you experience the positive effects of physical activity on your mood and state of mind (which the

Activity Trackers in this chapter can help you realize), you will be more likely to continue. Any weight loss, muscular toning, and flexibility you achieve is somewhat secondary to your goal of preventing bipolar relapse. If you lose weight, improve your appearance, or increase your strength and endurance, then that is a bonus to your primary goal, a very motivating bonus that is good for your overall health.

You are more likely to succeed when you plan for success, and the sections that follow in this chapter will help you make a plan that works for you and suits your lifestyle and level of physical health. It will focus on things you like to do and therefore are more likely to do. One way of having success is to join a fundraising effort where you raise funds for a charity by completing a specific physical activity goal. You will stay motivated and will have a concrete achievement at the end of a specific time period, such as three months or six months.

BIPOLAR SYMPTOMS

Because of the instability and severity of mood that often characterize bipolar disorder, many people with bipolar disorder find it hard to maintain a regular exercise routine.

When you are manic or hypomanic, you may feel really energized even if you are irritable—for example, if you are experiencing a mixed episode. If you begin to experience manic or hypomanic symptoms, physical activity can help you burn off some of that energy, reduce any "edginess" that you feel, improve your mood, and improve your concentration. In other words, now is the time to burn some calories. If you tend to lose your appetite when you have manic symptoms, do not forget to eat regularly so that your nutrition does not suffer and so that you do not drop below a healthy weight.

When you are depressed, it may feel like a workout just to get out of bed in the morning; but if you make physical activity a habit, just like brushing your teeth, it will be easier for you to keep it up no matter how depressed you are. You may find that even when you are depressed, your exercise is the one thing that you can complete for that day, and that is something to feel good about. You may also find that once you are out of bed and being active, you are less likely to return to bed and your symptoms may be alleviated.

You may not be able to do as much physical activity as usual when you are depressed, but you can make an effort. For example, if you normally walk a mile or two every day, even if walking around the block is all you can handle when you are depressed, just getting out of the house will make you feel better. At a time when you feel like you can do nothing, simply doing something, no matter how small, will have a positive effect on your mood and physical well-being. When you are depressed is not the time to set the goal of running a marathon (unless that will motivate you); rather the goal is to get out of bed, or off the sofa, or out from in front of the television, and try to do a little more each day than you did the day before.

Being sedentary does not feel good, does not do your body good, and keeps you in a depressed state. It may be very difficult to start moving, but it will ultimately improve your mood and make you less likely to become ill, because exercise boosts your immune system (which depression weakens). Even if you are sitting on the couch, you can do leg raises. Or if you do not want to face the world, you can walk the hallway of your home or walk the stairs in your building. If you have a dog, then taking your dog for a walk will get you out of the house for at least a few minutes each day. Whatever you do, it will be better than just sitting or lying there.

One of the ways you can increase the likelihood of continuing or beginning an exercise program when you are feeling manic or depressed is to enlist the support of an "exercise buddy" (see above)—or, if you can afford one, a personal trainer. This person can help you stay on track with your program of physical activity when you might be distracted from it due to manic symptoms and encourage you to follow through with planned exercise even when you do not feel like it due to depressive symptoms.

Having someone with whom you exercise will give you a sense of responsibility to this person as well as to yourself. You may want to give this person permission to call you if you do not show up for an exercise session or to call you beforehand to make sure you show up. It would also be a good idea to check in with this person before you make any decision to purchase exercise equipment, workout clothing, gym memberships, and so on, because when you are feeling manic or hypomanic you may be tempted to buy things that you do not really need or will not use.

HOW MUCH PHYSICAL ACTIVITY IS ENOUGH?

As I have stated, you do not necessarily need to engage in vigorous exercise to stay healthy and help prevent bipolar relapse. Most people walk every day without thinking of it as exercise, but every step you take helps keep your mood stable and your heart and lungs happy. Many sources consider a daily total of ten thousand steps (or about six miles) to constitute an active lifestyle, while less than five thousand steps is considered a sedentary lifestyle. Taking six thousand steps or more per day is considered somewhat active and can lengthen your lifespan, and more than ten thousand steps per day can help you lose weight (Tudor-Locke and Bassett 2004).

The Surgeon General's report titled *Physical Activity and Health* (1996) cites a recommendation from the Centers for Disease Control and Prevention and the American College of Sports Medicine (Pate et al. 1995) that uses somewhat different terms, stating that all adults should "accumulate" (i.e., do it over the course of the day, not necessarily all at once) thirty minutes of moderate-intensity activity on most, if not all, days of the week. Moderate intensity refers to feeling warm and slightly out of breath but still able to carry on a conversation, or, according to the UK's National Health Service (2013), breaking a sweat, elevating your heart rate, and increasing your breathing to the point of being unable to sing the words to a song. (The following website from the National Institutes of Health provides great examples of chores and sporting activities that provide a moderate level of exercise: http://www.nhlbi.nih.gov/hbp/prevent/p_active/m_1_phys.htm.) Walking briskly, riding a bike, swimming, and light running are considered moderate-intensity activities. Note that losing weight, which may be part of your bipolar illness management plan—especially due to weight gain that is a side effect of many medications—may require longer, more intense periods of exercise.

For people with bipolar disorder, the focus is on feeling well and preventing bipolar relapse, so the generally recommended amount of exercise is a good start, but you need to focus on what is right for you. You need the amount of physical activity that makes you feel healthy, reduces the impact of stress in your life, helps you maintain a healthy weight, and keeps depression and mania at bay. This differs for each person and may be much more than the minimum suggested by the surgeon general. The tracking tools in the next section will help you determine the level of activity that will keep your bipolar symptoms at bay.

One study found that the brain functioning of individuals with bipolar disorder was affected differently by obesity (a clinical condition), excess weight (a few extra pounds), and abdominal obesity (fat concentrated around the middle) (Alsuwaidan et al. 2009). In trying to explain the way that exercise works on brain function, the researchers proposed that exercise influences the systems of the brain that control metabolism, the immune system, and the propensity for inflammation. The researchers suggest that there needs to be more research about how much exercise is needed to have the positive impact on mood that exercise offers with regard to the psychiatric and physical health of people living with bipolar disorder.

Remember to consult your medical provider before you begin any exercise program or if you intend to significantly change your level of physical activity. You may have medical conditions that need to be taken into account when planning your physical activity, or your doctor may suggest that you focus on certain areas. If you set a goal of completing a 5k/10k, marathon, triathlon, or other goal and tie it to a fundraiser, you will find that you are being very physically active, you have a group of people who support and motivate you, and you have a performance challenge that will make you feel great when you complete it.

TRACKING YOUR PHYSICAL ACTIVITY AND YOUR MOOD

How much you move is often a sign of your mood. For example, you may be much more likely to be active when you are feeling hypomanic or manic and much less likely to move when you are depressed. In other words, your level of activity may be a clue to your mood, and your mood may be dependent on your level of activity.

If you have an exercise plan currently, the first chart below (also available at http://www.newharbinger.com/28814) will give you a baseline measure for your activity level. You should fill it out on a daily basis for at least two weeks (preferably a month). You can have several entries per day or none at all, depending on how active you are. The goal at this point, as you can see, is not to count calories burned or even measure your heart rate, but to focus on tracking your activity level and how you feel in response to exercising.

If you do not have an exercise plan currently, I suggest you get a pedometer to track how many steps you take throughout the day as an easy way to keep track of your total activity for the day. If you go this route, use the second chart below (also available at http://www.newharbinger.com/28814) and know that one minute of bicycling or swimming, if you do either of these activities, is the equivalent of 150 steps. I myself use the free app called *Moves* on my smartphone to track the number of steps I take during the day. It is easy to use, it is inconspicuous, and because I always keep my phone with me, I do not have to worry about remembering to wear a pedometer. Sometimes knowing that you will be tracking your behavior has an effect on your behavior. I find that if I monitor my number of steps, I do things that will increase the amount of steps I take: I walk rather than drive short distances; run errands I was planning to do on another day; or add a short walk to my day to reach my daily goal of 10,000 steps. I do not always achieve this goal, but it keeps me motivated and active and conscious of my level of physical activity.

You may find, as I do, that monitoring and tracking your physical activity is one way of increasing your likelihood of doing physical activity. For example, you may get to the point where you want to make sure you have done something to write in your Activity Tracker because you do not want it to be a sea of empty space. Because every little bit counts in getting you moving, just increasing the amount of steps you take each day is a move in the right direction. You need to track your activity for only one month to get you in the habit; when you get a steady routine going, you can use the Weekly Triggers and Mood Chart from chapter 2 to track whether or not you got enough exercise for the day (under "Healthy Behaviors"). But if physical activity will be a key part of your wellness plan, then buying an exercise journal from your local bookstore or sporting goods store or downloading pages you can use for the purpose (see the resources at the end of this chapter) may be well worth it.

Linking your mood to your activities will motivate you to do the types of activity, and get the level of activity, you need to keep your mood stable and stave off the extremes of depression and mania. For consistency, use the levels of mania and depression described in the Mood Rating Scale (see chapter 2 or visit the publisher's website for this book at http://www.newharbinger.com/28814).

WEEKLY ACTIVITY TRACKER 1

Day & Date	Mood Before	Beginning Time	Ending Time	Activity	Location	Mood After
Monday, _____						
Tuesday, _____						
Wednesday, _____						
Thursday, _____						
Friday, _____						
Saturday, _____						
Sunday, _____						

After entering the date, record your mood before starting your activity, using the Mood Rating Scale (write "depression" or "mania" and note intensity, or write "0"). Then record the time at which you start and end your activity, what activity you did, and where you did it. Finally, record how you felt afterward, again using the Mood Rating Scale. You may find that certain activities are more effective in lifting your mood or that certain times of the day work best for you. The goal of tracking and monitoring your mood along with your physical activity is to find the time, activity, and location that are most effective for improving or stabilizing your mood. The better your mood, the less likely you are to experience bipolar relapse.

WEEKLY ACTIVITY TRACKER 2: STEP TRACKER

Day & Date	Mood at the Beginning of the Day	Total Steps Taken	Mood at the End of the Day
Monday, _____			
Tuesday, _____			
Wednesday, _____			
Thursday, _____			
Friday, _____			
Saturday, _____			
Sunday, _____			

EVALUATING YOUR LEVEL OF PHYSICAL ACTIVITY

Once you have tracked your level of physical activity for at least a month, take stock of how your level of exercise compares to the recommended level of exercise. If you are already getting enough exercise, you may choose to simply keep doing what you are doing, or you may choose to increase the frequency or duration of your exercise (or the number of steps you take per day) in order to meet other goals, such as an increased fitness level or a weight loss goal. An hour of exercise per day will help you lose weight. Increase your activity level slowly, to make sure you can handle it and to avoid burnout.

If you are not getting enough physical activity—for example, if you are below the magic number of ten thousand steps a day—the rest of this chapter will help you develop a plan that works for you. In your plan, you should specify where you will exercise, how you will exercise, and when you will exercise. The more concrete your plan, the easier it will be to stick to it, because you will be prepared. Use the information from your Activity Tracker to help you set goals for slowly increasing your physical activity—for example, by one thousand steps per week. If you have the services of a personal trainer or are taking classes at a gym, include these activities as part of your plan.

DESIGNING AN EXERCISE PLAN

When you want to bring about any sort of changes in your life, creating a plan is a good way of helping you make those changes. It also helps you track and monitor your progress. Remember not to start any new exercise program without first checking with your medical provider. You may also want to consult a personal trainer to help you design a program that focuses on the results you want, even if you do not plan to use a personal trainer on a regular basis. Setting a goal such as completing a 5k or 10k run or walk, a marathon, or a triathlon, or participating in a fundraiser, may help keep you motivated and will also give you a specific plan to follow to achieve your goal.

WHERE YOU WILL EXERCISE

For some people, the right place for physical activity makes all the difference to getting regular exercise. For example, I have lived in the San Francisco Bay Area and in Seattle, and in both places I found it psychologically and emotionally soothing to walk around a lake (Lake Merritt and Green Lake, respectively). Because I did not have to count laps—I just walked around the lake once (approximately 5k) or twice (10k)—I could mentally relax and enjoy the scenery while my legs moved on "automatic pilot." This made it easy to get my physical activity done. I could start at any point along the lake—wherever I found parking—and then return to my car at the end of my walk. My morning walks by the lake were the best, because it was quiet, the fog was rising off the water, and the sun was rising. It was a beautiful place to be in motion and a peaceful way to start my day.

To encourage my habit and reduce barriers to consistency, I kept a change of clothes—sneakers, socks, a raincoat, a long-sleeve top, exercise pants, and a fleece jacket—in the car so that I could go to the lake at any time that suited my schedule, regardless of what I was wearing (I changed in the car if I had to). This made it easier for me to find time to walk and gave me no excuses for not having the proper clothes when I had the time. And because it was a simple 5k loop, my program of activity was consistent. My scenic walk has become a ritual—part of my daily routine, like eating, such that without it, I am not at my best. Your ideal backdrop for a walk may involve hiking a nature trail, walking to and from work, walking to the grocery store, or walking around the mall. It is your choice, based on what is available to you in your neighborhood and in your lifestyle.

Keep in mind that the easier it is for you to get to wherever you like to do your physical activity, the easier it will be to make it a habit. The more complicated it makes your routine, the less likely you are to incorporate it into your lifestyle. If you make getting physical activity a habit, then it becomes less of a chore and just part of your healthy lifestyle that prevents the recurrence of bipolar symptoms.

One way to make exercise part of your routine is to take several walking trips to the grocery store each week. This way, your bags will be light every time, you can buy fresh fruits and vegetables closer to the time you will eat them, and you will not keep too much food on hand that may tempt you to break your healthy routine. (Call it the French way, because people in France tend to make frequent trips to the grocery store to eat more fresh foods.)

Another way to get more physical activity is to try to make your appointments within walking distance of your place of employment or residence (especially if you live or work in a city) so that you can walk to your errands. You not only will save money on gas and parking, but you may find that by the time you get your car and find parking on both trips, it may have been just as efficient to walk, especially if the distance is less than a mile. Yet another option, if you have a favorite tourist attraction or historic neighborhood in your town or city, is to give daily walking tours (on a paid or volunteer basis). Walking to visit a friend or to go to a place of worship is also a good way to incorporate exercise with your social support system.

Some people really enjoy spending time in indoor or outdoor pools. The repetitiveness of swimming laps, combined with the Zen-like experience of being in the water, calms not only their body but also their mind. Other people prefer the serenity of a yoga studio. Note that you may wish to exercise indoors so that you will not be deterred by weather, but there is benefit to doing physical activity outside. Remember that sunlight is important for mood regulation, as was discussed in the section on circadian rhythms and sleep in chapter 3. (And it need not be a sunny day for you to enjoy the benefits of sunlight, because the sun's rays can often come through on a hazy day.) You can maximize the benefits of your physical activity program by being active outside, where the fresh air and even the smallest bit of sunlight can elevate your mood immediately.

Some people like the comfort of home because they are not comfortable doing physical activity in the presence of other people. That is also perfectly fine. What matters is that you find a place where you can consistently enjoy your physical activity of choice in a manner that is convenient to you and suitable to your lifestyle.

HOW YOU WILL EXERCISE

For many people, the hardest part of deciding on a program of exercise is choosing an activity that they will love to do come rain, shine, heat, or cold. What kind of exercise is best? The answer is whatever physical activity you like to do is best for you. There is no "best" for everyone, because if you hate what you are doing, you will not maintain your program of exercise. Therefore, carefully consider your likes, dislikes, budget, location, and lifestyle.

My favorite activity is walking because it requires little special equipment (a comfortable pair of walking shoes or sneakers), because I can do it anytime and anywhere, and because it allows me to enjoy the outdoors. Being outside really helps lift my mood when I am feeling down and calms me when I am feeling hypomanic. I can also determine how far I want to go and go at my own pace. Sometimes I have what I call "destination walks": for example, I will walk to a grocery store and then take the bus back or walk back with my groceries in a backpack. I also use my walks as "medication." If I am feeling down, I get out and walk, or if I need to "take the edge off," I go for a walk. Sometimes that may mean walking first thing in the morning (which always makes my day seem brighter and helps me sleep better at night) or on my lunch break instead of sitting at my desk.

If you feel overwhelmed by all the choices available to you, think of them as a buffet and try different physical activities until you find what is right for you. This may take some time and some money, but often gyms and fitness studios offer free trials, and that can be your way to get some exercise while saving on costs and helping you find the activity that may eventually become part of your daily routine. For best results, try to settle on something that is easy—or at least not very difficult—to incorporate into your schedule and current lifestyle. The fewer barriers to your participation there are, the more likely you are to do what you should do and the longer you are likely to stay with it.

If you cannot think of ways to get started on a program of physical activity, it may be worth investing in a fitness book or DVD or at least one session with a personal trainer (sometimes the first session is free) who can construct a fitness routine that fits with your physical activity goals, your budget, and your lifestyle.

Whatever you choose to do, get active and stay active. The secret to maintaining an active lifestyle is to find activities that you love to do and do them as much as you can. Following are some physical activities that you might find enjoyable that you can schedule into your week.

- Take a dance class or use an exercise video or DVD.

- Go dancing with friends.

- While your child is playing soccer or any other sport, walk around the field (or the court if you can).

- Take a walking "date" with a loved one instead of sitting over a glass of wine or a cup of tea or coffee.

- Take a hike. This does not require that you go into the mountains. Simply walk through a park or take an urban hike by finding an interesting route in town and walking along it briskly.

- Join a fundraising program (such as for breast cancer research) that requires you to join a group of people who have a physical activity goal.

- Visit an art gallery or museum, and take in as many exhibits as you can.

WHEN YOU WILL EXERCISE

Next, consider the times of day that would work best for increasing your activity level. If you have regularly scheduled meetings with a coworker, instead of sitting across a table from each other, perhaps you can discuss the day's business over a walk instead. People often find it easier to be creative and to engage intellectually while moving. Any time you can take fifteen minutes is a good time to schedule some physical activity. A swim may be inconvenient in the middle of the day, but a fifteen-minute walk may be feasible as a way of breaking up your day. For example, after arriving at work you may spend an hour checking e-mail, then walk for fifteen minutes, then return to your desk to work on administrative tasks. After finishing those tasks, you may take another fifteen-minute walk to deliver some office mail or to do the coffee run for your office. At lunchtime you may walk for fifteen minutes, eat a healthy lunch, then walk for another fifteen minutes. In this way, by the end of lunchtime you will have walked for an hour total.

You may choose to take public transit to and from work as a way to incorporate walking into your routine at the beginning and end of your day. Not only will you be getting more exercise, but you may find it convenient to do some work, learn a new language, or listen to an audiobook on the bus or train, and it will probably be less stressful than driving.

STRATEGIES FOR INCREASING YOUR ACTIVITY LEVEL EVEN FURTHER

You should also include in your exercise plan at least one way to get more physical activity on an informal basis. I have already touched on some of these strategies in this chapter. Many require only a couple of minutes, so there is no need to schedule them, but you should keep them in mind as you go about your day. Others you can do as the opportunity arises. Add one of the following recommendations to your exercise plan, or come up with your own, and see how it goes for one week. If it does not work for you, then try something else. The goal is to find a routine and stick with it.

- Park your car farther from the door when running errands, going shopping, or visiting friends.

- Take the stairs instead of the elevator.

- Take your dog for longer walks.

- Walk the extra distance to or from bus or train stops that are farther away.

- Do some stretches, weightlifting, or walking or marching in place during the commercial breaks of your favorite TV show or as a break at work.

- At work, use the most out-of-the-way bathroom, photocopier, or watercooler to add some distance to your daily total.

- Hand deliver items to your coworkers instead of sending them through interoffice mail.

- Choose to have work-related meetings in locations you can walk to from your office so that you get to walk to the meeting instead of the person coming to your office.

- Forget about the drive-through window; park the car and walk into the building.

- Take 10- to 15-minute walk breaks every hour or two at work. Your productivity will actually increase, because exercise improves mental performance. (Your brain will be clearer and more efficient.) This will also reduce stress and give your body a break from its routine.

- Do your errands and commuting on foot or bicycle instead of driving. (You may want to add a basket or other carriers to your bicycle.)

- Tour open homes and enjoy your hobbies by going to trade shows and walking as much of the showroom floor as possible.

- Get up from your sofa and use the buttons on your TV instead of using the remote control.

- Do less sitting: If you have a desk job, get up and move around at least every hour.

  If you take a five- to fifteen-minute walk every hour at work, you will have accumulated a total of at least thirty-five minutes of activity and a lot of steps by the end of an eight-hour day.

- Learn to do DIY (do-it-yourself) projects at home.

  You will learn a new skill, feel great about saving money and creating the home you want, and burn a few calories.

- Wash your car yourself instead of going through an automated car wash. You will keep your paint job shiny, save money, and increase your level of activity.

- Keep a good pair of walking shoes, a rain poncho, a workout top, and some socks in your car so that, like me, you are always prepared to take a walk or run if you have the opportunity, no matter the weather.

  If I am driving and find myself with some time, I pull over at the nearest park or a paved path and take a walk. It is invigorating and just one more thing you can say you did to get more physical activity at the end of the day.

- Lastly, if you have a pet, make it a plan to get your pet in good physical condition by taking him or her along for your walk or run.

Following is a sample Weekly Exercise Plan and one for you to fill out (which is also also available at http://www.newharbinger.com /28814).

SAMPLE WEEKLY EXERCISE PLAN

Date range: 6/15/13 - 6/21/13	**Where/How/When**
Mon.	Walk nature trail, 7:00 a.m.
Tues.	Swim at local pool after work
Wed.	Walk for half hour at lunchtime
Thurs.	Rest day
Fri.	Walk nature trail at 7:00 a.m.
Sat.	Go for a walk with a friend
Sun.	Go for a bike ride along a bike trail

WEEKLY EXERCISE PLAN

Date range: _____ – _____ Goal for this week: _____	
Mon.	
Tues.	
Wed.	
Thurs.	
Fri.	
Sat.	
Sun.	

Strategy/strategies: _____

Comments: _____

Remember, the key is to increase your physical activity slowly and steadily. No matter what activities you choose to start with, be patient with yourself and do not push yourself to do too much at once. If you normally walk for ten minutes a day and you choose to walk more, for example, you can walk for fifteen minutes a day the first week, twenty minutes a day the second week, and so on. If you are riding a bicycle or rollerblading, your goals may involve longer distance instead of time.

However you choose to do it, set goals that you can attain and reward yourself for achieving them.

RESOURCES

Following are a couple more charts you can use to help you plan and track your activity in more detail.

- Vertex42's "Exercise Chart" (http://www.vertex42.com /ExcelTemplates/Images/printable-exercise-chart_large.gif)

  This chart contains sections for warm-up, cooldown, cardio, and strength training.

- MerckEngage.com's "Daily Planner" (free, but requires you to create a username and password) (https://www.merck engage.com/01_plan/daily-planner/view-day.aspx)

  This comprehensive online tracking and monitoring program allow you to create a meal plan (with calorie information) as well as a fitness plan.

SUMMARY

Regular exercise has multiple benefits for everyone, regardless of their mental state. The physical benefits include lower risk for heart disease, hypertension, and diabetes, as well as improved flexibility and strength. The weight gain that is a side effect of some bipolar medications can also be minimized with a program of regular physical activity. The mental benefits of exercise include improved mood, better brain function, and more satisfying sleep. You can maximize these mental health benefits if you exercise outdoors, especially in sunlight.

No matter what sort of physical activity you choose to do, do it often and do it consistently to keep your mood stable and reduce the likelihood of bipolar relapse.

CHAPTER 6

PEOPLE

People are the fourth and final component of the SNAP approach to preventing bipolar relapse. As readers of my last book, *Bipolar 101*—from which elements of this chapter have been adapted—will recognize, building and maintaining positive interpersonal relationships and creating a network of social support that includes family, friends, mental health care professionals, colleagues, support group members, exercise buddies, and others is important for several reasons:

- People are a part of the world around you, and staying engaged with the world around you can keep depression at bay.

- Spending time with people whose company you enjoy can increase your happiness, or your level of mental well-being.

- The more time you spend with people to whom you have disclosed your bipolar disorder, the better able they will be to let you know when you seem to be exhibiting symptoms that may precede a mood episode.

- Reducing problems in your relationships with loved ones or people at work can help you avoid stress that might trigger a relapse.

- If you have support in dealing with stress and other triggers, your risk of bipolar relapse will be lower.

- Mutual trust and open communication with your mental health care provider will enable you to get the help you need when you need it and develop a program of health maintenance that keeps you from relapsing.

You do not have to take my word for it. Studies show that a supportive social network is beneficial for people with bipolar disorder. Social support, along with medication adherence and psychotherapy, keeps bipolar symptoms from becoming very serious and reduces the risk of bipolar relapse and the risk of suicide (Altman et al. 2006). The more social strain people with bipolar disorder experience (Eidelman et al. 2012), or the lower their levels of perceived social support (Pratchett 2010), the worse their bipolar symptoms will be. Social support is even associated with better sleep in people with bipolar disorder (Eidelman et al. 2012). Unsupportive social networks, on the other hand, have been found to increase the likelihood of medication non-adherence (Sajatovic et al. 2006) and thus may negatively affect the course of mental illness.

Maintaining your social support system to reduce your symptoms requires your active participation in your relationships and demands a great degree of sensitivity when you are symptomatic and may alienate people close to you. Some do's for maintaining good relationships include:

Stay in touch by phone, e-mail, or text with regular communication (depending on the closeness of the relationship, weekly or monthly, for example).

Meet with your loved ones on as regular a social basis as possible, depending on your schedule and theirs.

Maintain the mutuality of your relationships so that you are neither always the one giving nor always the one getting.

Communicate kindly and gently. Avoid serious conversations when you are depressed, and make no promises when you are hypomanic.

For adolescents with bipolar disorder, it appears that family relationships play a role in the onset and continuation of bipolar symptoms (Sullivan et al. 2012): family conflict, lack of adaptability, and lack of cohesion are predictors of adolescent mood symptoms. For this reason, the authors of the study cited suggested that family conflict be a focus of psychosocial intervention in early onset bipolar disorder.

THE FIRST PERSON IS YOU

The first person you need to focus on is you. To become comfortable with being ill is to become at ease with taking steps to be, and stay, healthy. If you are not committed to your own mental wellness, then it will be difficult for other people to support you. But when you believe in your ability to be well, other people will want to support you. There are three common beliefs you must counteract when working on your own attitudes toward your illness. These beliefs fuel the stigma against mental illness and are also the result of stigma.

First, *your bipolar disorder is not your fault.* However, you do have some control over your symptoms—how often they occur and how severe they are. You also have some control over how long they last. The goal is to have fewer, less severe, and shorter mood episodes. You have to believe that you have some power over your bipolar disorder in order for you to take steps to stabilize your mood and for you to maintain healthy habits once you start.

Second, *having bipolar disorder does not make you weak or incompetent, nor does it make you a failure.* It is simply an illness that requires proactive behaviors if you are to stay well. These include taking your medications as prescribed and having regular visits with a mental health care professional. Because bipolar disorder is a cyclical, chronic illness, it is easy to feel "healthy" when you are not symptomatic and then feel out of control when you are ill. Know that whether you are sick or well, you always have some control over your bipolar disorder. Again, you have to believe that you do in order for you to take control.

Third, *bipolar disorder is not who you are—it is an illness you have.* There is more to you than an illness of the brain. It is important to find time to do things you love so that you see yourself in a much broader context. Instead of focusing only on your symptoms and management of your illness, participate in activities that you love and spend time with people you care about. Indulge the passions that make you happy. Learn new hobbies, take courses, travel, participate in physical activities.

You *are not* "bipolar"; you *have* bipolar disorder. It is an illness that influences your mood and your behavior, but it is not the only determinant of your personality or your experience of the world. As you read in previous chapters, your willingness to eat well, take your medications, monitor and track your mood and triggers, and live a physically active lifestyle all influence how much bipolar disorder affects you.

TYPES OF SUPPORT

There are many types of support that can help you prevent bipolar relapse—many ways that other people can help you maintain a healthy lifestyle, reduce your triggers, and minimize your symptoms of bipolar disorder. They include emotional support, group support, material support, treatment support, financial support, employer support, and crisis support. Support can look like accompanying you to health care visits, being an exercise partner, notifying your employer if you get hospitalized or are ill, or supporting you in your maintenance plan. Ideally, all of these types of support involve relationships with people who are significant to you so that the support they provide has meaning and power.

EMOTIONAL SUPPORT

Emotional support means an ear when you need one and a shoulder to lean on. Emotional support is best sought from someone who knows you well, understands bipolar disorder, and will not judge you for needing support. Having someone to call in the middle of the night when you are feeling afraid or anxious or simply cannot sleep is what having good emotional support looks like. You may seek emotional support at different times from different people: a family member, a friend, the on-call nurse of your HMO, or the counselor on the other end of a mental health hotline. The members of your emotional support system are there to help you when you need someone to support you in your maintenance plan, talk with you about your joys and your sorrows, and help celebrate your victories. They may also support you by accompanying you to medical visits. And they are basically loved ones who love you when you need loving.

GROUP SUPPORT

Group support from other people who have bipolar disorder or another mental disorder can really help you feel that you are not alone. Members of a support group—whether it is formal or informal, online or offline—can be valuable sources of information about bipolar disorder and ideas for maintaining your health. These people can answer questions you may have about bipolar symptoms or about the side effects of medication. They can help you stick to your medication and provide general support for maintaining a healthy lifestyle, encouraging positive behaviors that keep you from relapsing.

MATERIAL SUPPORT

Material support consists of help with activities like taking care of your home, your children, or your pets when you are in crisis or if you are trying to stave off a relapse at a time when you are feeling vulnerable. Perhaps you have a nanny, babysitter, housekeeper, or pet sitter who can be ready to take over any time you are not able to carry out your daily responsibilities or when you are trying to reduce your commitments in order to focus on your health. Friends, family, and professionals all can be sources of material support.

TREATMENT SUPPORT

Treatment support involves encouragement to follow your treatment plan as outlined by your mental health care provider, as well as encouragement to follow the recommendations regarding sleep, nutrition, and activity in this book.

Support groups of any kind are a great place to find support for following your treatment plan. Your psychotherapist and other health care providers are also good sources of support for maintaining your treatment plan. If you are quitting nicotine, caffeine, or alcohol, your friends, family, or medical providers can support you in these efforts to practice healthy behaviors. Explain to anyone who encourages you to have "just one" cigarette, drink of alcohol, or cup of java why you are abstaining and why it is so important to your overall health and your mental health. You must believe that your health should be paramount in order to convince others to support you in maintaining it.

FINANCIAL SUPPORT

You may need financial support to cover the cost of medications or psychotherapy. If there is someone out there who knows your situation and with whom you have a relationship of trust, you may want to ask whether this person would help pay for things that are part of your bipolar relapse prevention strategies.

Whether you are in debt or not, another way to improve your financial situation is to consult a personal finance expert, who can help you reduce your spending and become a better money manager. If you can reduce the stress that comes with financial problems, you will also reduce your risk of relapse.

Some people with bipolar disorder shop a lot when they are manic or when they are depressed. Finding support for a good financial plan will help you reduce the risk of getting in trouble financially when you are symptomatic.

EMPLOYER SUPPORT

Although the risk of stigma or the potential consequences of telling people at work about your bipolar disorder may make you choose other avenues for support, employer support can help you preserve your reputation at work and maximize your productivity without risking your mental health. Employer support refers to reasonable accommodations, to which people with mental illness are entitled under the Americans with Disabilities Act (ADA), that will help you perform at your best.

It may be hard to tell your boss about your illness, and it may be best to test the waters before you open up fully by seeing how your colleagues react to discussions about mental illness in general. If you are a student at college or high school, you may want to share your diagnosis with a school counselor, your academic advisor, or a trusted teacher so that this person can help you manage your course load and maximize your academic success.

One strategy is to tell your boss when you are doing well at work so that the image he or she has of you is one of competence and not one of deficiency. This way, when you need help, you have already set a high standard of your performance against which you can be measured. Again, you have rights under the Americans with Disabilities Act (ADA), and the U.S. Equal Employment Opportunities Commission (EEOC) is the place to go if you feel you are being discriminated against because of your mental illness. You can find information on both the EEOC and the ADA at the EEOC's "Facts About the Americans with Disabilities Act" web page (http://www.eeoc.gov/facts/fs-ada.html).

You may choose to tell your company's human resources department about your bipolar disorder instead of your immediate supervisor. That way, key people in the organization are aware of your problem but it is less likely to influence your relationship with your direct supervisor.

CRISIS SUPPORT

Crisis support is the kind of support you need when things are not going well or you find yourself in an episode. In a crisis situation, you may require many different forms of support on very short notice at any time of day or night. The kind of person from whom you should seek crisis support is someone who is dependable and has previously agreed to provide this kind of support. It is good to have a small group of people who have agreed to help you if ever you are in a state of crisis so that you do not burden one person, who may or may not be available in the moment to help you with the responsibility. Furthermore, different people may agree to provide different kinds of support if you need it. The person who talks you through dark thoughts in the middle of the night may be different than the one who comes over and keeps you company or helps you with your family obligations.

CREATING A SOCIAL SUPPORT NETWORK

You may already have an extensive social support network without being aware of it, or you may have to consciously seek out people who can help you stay well. It is important to be deliberate in your efforts to build a network of people who can support your mental health and be there for you in case of an emergency. You will need to inform people of your bipolar disorder and how they can help. Try to surround yourself with positive people who lift you up when you need it, and avoid people who are judgmental or are not willing to learn about your illness. People who do not understand bipolar disorder, or are not willing to learn, may sabotage your efforts to be healthy or misinterpret some of your symptoms and make it more difficult for you to get support.

YOUR MEDICAL AND MENTAL HEALTH CARE TEAM

Your medical and mental health care providers are an important part of your social support network. Not only do they work with you to develop and adjust your treatment plan as necessary—having a professional to call in a crisis can really make a difference, even save your life—but they can also be a resource in building your social support system. If you are in counseling, you may choose to use your counseling sessions to develop a plan and strategy for telling people about your mental illness. You can use your time in session to practice what you are going to say. You may also arrange to have your mental health care provider mediate your conversations with loved ones such as your spouse, partner, or child. Your therapist may help you structure your conversation so that both parties feel heard, as well as help you answer any questions your loved one has. Your loved one can then ask your provider general questions about the disorder and how to become an integral part of your support system.

Your medical provider can also help you decide whether you need a medical advance directive in case you need to be hospitalized against your will. A medical advance directive is a living will or durable power of attorney for health care. In this document, you give directions about future medical care you are likely to receive. In this case, your medical advance directive would include specific directions for the type of medical care you want to receive specific to your bipolar disorder. Lastly, you may consult your health care provider about who should have access to your health care information in case you are having debilitating symptoms and need care. Typically, the people who have this type of access are parents, spouses or domestic partners, or close and trustworthy friends.

Including others in your social support network in your treatment is something you should discuss with your health care providers. They can help you decide who would be best to accompany you to therapy sessions, medical appointments, or support group meetings and who would be best to ask for various other types of support.

Write down the contact information for your primary care providers and mental health care team. You may want to give this information to the other people you will identify as members of your social support network so that if they have concerns about your mental health they have someone to whom they can turn for advice or to seek help for you. You may also want to include at least partial contact information on an emergency card (or piece of paper) in your wallet, to keep with you at all times, for when you need help fast (see "Your Crisis Plan"). A card for your use is provided on the next page (and online at http://www .newharbinger.com/28814).

YOUR HEALTH CARE PROVIDERS

Name	Profession	Phone	E-mail	Address

TELLING OTHERS ABOUT YOUR BIPOLAR DISORDER

The first step in getting support beyond your health care providers is to tell people that you have bipolar disorder. It is not necessary to tell everyone in your life about your bipolar disorder. For example, people with whom you have little contact or a passing relationship do not need to know, unless your illness is likely to affect them directly. The people who should know about your bipolar disorder are those closest to you who have experienced, or will experience, the impact of your illness, and are likely to be supportive. For example, people you share a home with will be impacted by your symptoms and should know that you have bipolar disorder and how it may influence your relationships. People who are close to you and who are important to you should also know about how your bipolar disorder may impact the relationship.

Depending on the circumstances, this may include your romantic partner, your parents, your siblings, your children, your friends, your coworkers, and your employer. It is only fair that these people understand why you may have behaved, or will behave, the way you do. Some may have difficulty processing what you are saying. Many people hold stereotypes about the mentally ill and may not be able to reconcile their image of you with their image of someone who is mentally ill, especially if you tell them about your illness when you are healthy (which I advise). However, the benefits of letting go of the secret, and stigma, of your illness is worth the risk of having some people not understand. You can view this as an opportunity to educate people about your illness, which in the long run will actually help reduce the stigma and discrimination you may face. In the process, you will learn who your "friends" really are. The people to choose as members of your support network will be those who are most understanding or who offer assistance when they learn of your illness.

It is best to tell people about your bipolar disorder when you are healthy so that they understand more clearly that you are not ill all the time and that your symptoms are cyclical. As mentioned, the person you are disclosing your illness to may have a hard time imagining you in your ill state and may dismiss your symptoms or the illness. Giving people a brochure or the address of a website that explains about mental illness in general, and bipolar disorder specifically (see "Eight Tips for Telling People About Your Bipolar Disorder," below), allows them to find out more information—on their own time, at their own pace— about this complex and sometimes confusing condition.

Anxiety About Disclosure

It is natural to feel anxious when telling someone that you have a chronic and severe illness. Telling people that you have bipolar disorder can be challenging—even scary. You may be ashamed of or uncomfortable with being ill. The stigma of having a mental disorder can make you fear rejection, judgment, or being viewed as weak or unable to cope with life. You may rather never tell anyone about your illness who does not already know.

However, not telling anyone about your bipolar disorder is *not* an option. Secrecy fosters isolation, which can sabotage your management of your symptoms because being alone and feeling isolated exacerbates triggers that may lead to a mood episode. Plus, it is more painful to suffer in silence. Remember that research shows that social support is important to any plan to get and stay well. Everyone needs a support system, because as the saying goes, "No [one] is an island."

So the first thing you need to do is get comfortable with having bipolar disorder. In other words, the first person who needs to be put at ease is you. Accepting your illness means coming to terms with the fact that you have a chronic, severe mental illness. If you have not already done so, you may need to talk with a mental health counselor about accepting the diagnosis and preparing for engaging in treatment. You may find it helpful to journal your feelings in the months after your diagnosis so that you can process your feelings about your struggles and living with the challenges of bipolar disorder.

Try some of the relaxation techniques you have learned to deal with this stressful situation. Deep breathing exercises and writing down what you want to say will help increase your confidence in facing this challenge. (See "Eight Tips for Telling People About Your Bipolar Disorder" later in this chapter for an example of how to get started.) Once you have a script, you may want to practice it on someone who already knows about your illness. If you have no one to practice with, you can practice in the mirror until you gain the confidence you need to initiate the conversation.

It is true that you may risk rejection, disappointment, and stigmatization even from people who care about you and are close to you. To prepare yourself for the possibility of a negative reaction, talk to your mental health care provider about strategies that will work for you or how you will cope if things go awry and you feel rejected, judged, or misunderstood. You may also want to consult the websites of the National Alliance on Mental Illness (http://www.nami.org) and the Depression and Bipolar Support Alliance (http://www.dbsalliance.org) for more advice on how to disclose your illness. Later in this chapter, you will find a few suggestions for responding to negativity when telling someone about your bipolar disorder.

Telling the Different Kinds of People in Your Life

Disclosure of your bipolar disorder is a kind of "coming out" and may present personal and practical challenges. It may test your relationships and cause you to question yourself and your identity. The following discussion outlines some ways and how much to tell the various people in your life about your illness (later in the chapter, we will cover how to ask for the support you need). As mentioned, the people you should share your illness with are those who are most important to you and with whom you interact on a regular basis.

Your romantic partner. If you have not already told your spouse, partner, girlfriend, boyfriend, or lover that you have bipolar disorder, do so as soon as possible. He or she has probably already noticed symptoms of your illness, so disclosure may help explain your behavior. I recommend that you share what the triggers for your bipolar symptoms are so that your romantic partner is aware of what events may bring on a mood episode and can help you manage your illness.

As part of this disclosure, you may want to discuss any sexual implications of the side effects of your medications or of your depressive or manic episodes. For example, some antidepressants and antipsychotic medications reduce sexual performance. Depression usually decreases your libido—most people who are depressed lose interest in sex. Conversely, one of the symptoms of mania is hypersexuality, which means a high libido and a desire to have multiple partners or have sex more often than usual.

If you are single at the moment, in the future, tell anyone you date about your bipolar disorder as soon as the relationship gets serious. This is not the kind of news to spring on someone after he or she has committed to a relationship with you, if you can help it. At the same time, it is usually neither appropriate nor helpful to disclose such facts on a first date; there is no point in making yourself vulnerable and spending a lot of time answering questions about your illness if the person may not be around in your life for long. Your future partner, however, should be aware of what he or she is "getting into" before making a relationship commitment. It is important to an open, honest relationship that you disclose your bipolar disorder. Not only is it better to spend your energy on preventing bipolar relapse than on trying to protect your mental health "secret" from the person closest to you, but also disclosure can get you some much-needed support. Telling your romantic partner about your bipolar disorder sooner rather than later may also save you from a broken heart down the road if he or she does not feel prepared to deal with the potential challenges of living with someone who has bipolar disorder.

Make a special time to have this conversation; avoid having it at dinner or bedtime, when your time is limited and there are distractions. If you have alienated your partner as a result of the behaviors associated with your illness, you may choose to tell him or her in front of a third party, such as a psychotherapist or a spiritual leader, who can help the two of you discuss some of the issues that may arise.

Open communication is key to healthy relationships. Relationships that stand the test of time are those in which couples acknowledge a wide range of feelings—from happiness to sadness to anger. Disclosing your illness may create tension in a relationship, but if you are willing to hear and understand how the other person feels, this two-way exchange will be the foundation for your "new" relationship, one that will be strong and lasting, in which this person is a member of your support network. When telling your partner about your illness, then, it is important to make time afterward to really talk about any fears and potential challenges to the relationship.

Your parents/siblings (family of origin). Depending on the relationships you have with your family members, you may decide to tell them all at once or one at a time. Consider how close your relationship is to each family member, how open you think he or she will be to hearing what you have to say, and how supportive he or she is likely to be. If you think that someone in particular may not be as supportive as the rest, then telling your family members as a group will allow him or her to see the support of the others and hopefully influence him or her to be more supportive or open to what you have to say. If you think that most of your family members will not be supportive at first, then it is best not to have to confront a group of people who may not be understanding and instead discuss your illness with someone who you think has influence within your family. Winning over someone who has influence may make your task easier when you decide to talk to other family members.

If everyone is willing, family therapy is a good option for both the short and long term—it helps ensure that past issues within your family will not get in the way of your getting and staying well. Family therapy may help your family members explore their feelings about your illness and understand both how it affects you and how they can be a part of your treatment plan. You may also discover that other people in your family have bipolar disorder since it is familial.

Your child. Your child should not be a member of your social support network unless he or she is an adult, but he or she should know something about your bipolar disorder nonetheless. Telling your child that you have a mental illness is a very difficult task and one that will vary according to the age of your child. The older your child is, the more details you can provide about your symptoms and treatment. You can also discuss with an older child how your symptoms may have affected him or her in the past. A young child, on the other hand, may simply need to know that you are sick but are taking steps to feel better. You may say something like "Mommy (or Daddy) is not feeling well but is going to the doctor to feel better." If you have had depression or manic symptoms, it is likely that your child has noticed these changes in you, and giving him or her a context in which to understand your behavior may help relieve any fear and confusion it has caused.

Be careful to avoid making your child feel responsible for your bipolar symptoms. For example, if you are depressed, your children should not have to cook and care for themselves or you or feel obligated to take care of the household because you are not able to do so. Reassure your child or children that you are getting treatment and will make sure that there will always be someone to take care of him or her. Encourage the sharing of feelings and questions. Apologize for any pain you may have caused during a mood episode, and assure your child that you are working hard not to have it happen again.

You may also want to strategize with your child about how you will communicate with him or her if you are experiencing any bipolar symptoms. You may want to share what to expect with regard to how you relate to him or her. When your child knows what to expect, he or she is less likely to feel afraid of your illness or to be disappointed when your symptoms prevent you from being the parent you usually are.

Your friends. My advice for telling your friends is similar to that for telling your family members. If your friends have already seen your mania or depression, you can explain to them why you behaved the way you did and how having bipolar disorder affects your life.

If you have a group of friends with whom you spend a lot of time, you may choose to have them over for dinner and tell them all at once—it can be your bipolar disorder "coming out" party. Bringing some light fun to your conversation will make it easier for you and for them. You may have a laugh at some of the situations that you have been in as a result of your bipolar disorder, while maintaining a serious conversation about the negative aspects of the illness. What may have seemed like a fun escapade to your friends may have been a manic episode, and helping them understand the nature of your illness will help them know when your "upbeat" mood may not be as healthy as it seems.

If you have friends who do not know each other, you will need to tell them one at a time. A good way to keep the conversation from feeling too heavy is to have it while you are out and about, perhaps on a walk together. Walking with a friend is a nice way to get some physical activity and provides the social connection and interaction that will minimize your risk of relapse. A good place to have this important conversation is in a park. Being outside is a mood lifter, and the tranquility provided by green space will reduce the stress that such a conversation may bring.

Your coworkers or employer. Before telling your coworkers or employer, you must consider carefully the implications it may have for your reputation, management's expectations of you, and your experience of stigma on the job. If you have had job-performance issues in the past, telling your employer about your bipolar disorder may shed light on these problems, but it may also make your employer think twice about your prospects. It is highly recommended that you become familiar with your rights and obligations under the Americans with Disabilities Act (ADA) and the Equal Employment Opportunities Commission (EEOC).

You may want to consult a lawyer prior to talking about your illness to anyone at your workplace, to help you understand the legal and financial implications of doing so. Also become familiar with your company's human resources policies so that you know the policies and procedures that may relate to your situation. You can inform a human resources professional (who will keep it confidential) about your bipolar disorder and ask for help strategizing how to tell your immediate supervisor. You can also take the opportunity to let your supervisor or human resources department know that you are actively seeking treatment so that your employer feels less concerned about how your illness will affect your performance.

You may choose to tell more than one of your managers or colleagues at the same time, to prevent you from having to repeat yourself and to ensure that this information is not disseminated in a manner you would not want it to be. Telling your story directly preserves your voice and allows you to include the details that you think are most important. Remember that under the Americans with Disabilities Act (ADA) you have the right to reasonable accommodations that will help improve your job performance. These accommodations may include changing your hours to help you get better sleep (as discussed in chapter 3, many people with bipolar disorder have problems with sleep). For example, if waking up in the morning leaves you feeling tired and vulnerable to bipolar symptoms, a later start time and a later departure time may help you improve your productivity at work. You may also want to ask for an arrangement that allows you to work from home with less responsibility when you are feeling depressed or manic so that you can still be productive while absent. You may also formally ask for "stress breaks," such as leaving your desk every hour or two to take a walk or to de-stress in any way that works for you.

Remember that some workplaces are a lot more flexible and open than others. Although it is illegal under the ADA for your employer to fire you because of your illness, if you feel that disclosure would create a stressful work environment or threaten your position, you may want to find work that is more conducive to the management of your bipolar disorder. You have no legal obligation to tell your employer before being hired, especially if you do not need accommodations right away. You may never need to tell your employer if you do not get symptomatic in a way that interrupts your work performance.

However, if you realize you are experiencing symptoms it is a good idea to consult your human resources department to be aware of policies and procedures. It is also a good idea to be aware of your legal rights before having a conversation with your employer if you need to take time off. You want to be proactive in finding ways to maintain your performance at work instead of putting your job at risk because you did not get the appropriate support. Having a conversation with your mental health provider about this process is a good way to start so that you can know what you need and for how long.

Eight Tips for Telling People About Your Bipolar Disorder

Because telling people about your bipolar disorder can be such a challenge, here is a list of tips that may help make the conversation easier and more productive for both parties. It is a good idea to explore these conversations with your mental health care provider so that you can get support and guidance in communication strategies that will make the best of these conversations.

1. As mentioned, start with the people closest to you whose lives may have been affected by your illness. They will appreciate knowing why you have behaved the way you have.

2. Consider telling people who have helped you in the past when you were experiencing symptoms but did not necessarily know that you had bipolar disorder. They are most likely to be helpful in the future, and they deserve an explanation for your behavior.

3. Wait a while to tell people you think will not be supportive or understanding. Having some success first at telling people who are more supportive will give you the strength to tell anyone who may be less supportive.

4. Find a time and place to talk that is calm and free of distractions. Public places where you can be overheard, such as a noisy restaurant or a café, are not good choices. However, going for a walk in the park or sitting on a park bench together may give you the level of privacy you need while giving you the open-air environment that may make it easier to share. For most people, the easiest way may be to invite the person (or people) to your home (or go to theirs) and keep the television and radio off. The safety and comfort of your home may make it easier for you to make yourself emotionally vulnerable. If you are telling your employer, ask to meet at a time when neither of you is likely to be interrupted for at least an hour, in a quiet office where the door can be closed.

5. Stick to simple facts about bipolar disorder, and briefly describe how bipolar disorder affects you. If your relationship is close, you may choose to start by saying how much you care about the other person and how much he or she means to you, and explain that this is why you have chosen to speak with him or her about your illness. If you have caused him or her any pain during one of your mood episodes, you may want to add an apology and explain that your behavior was a result of your illness.

6. One way to start the conversation is to say: "I would like to tell you something that is important to me and that may affect our relationship. It may have already affected our relationship in the past. When I am finished telling you, please feel free to ask any questions you may have. I am being treated for bipolar disorder, and I am working on staying healthy. Although I am healthy now, and planning to stay that way, bipolar disorder is a chronic but treatable condition that results in severe mood swings between depression and mania. This means that

sometimes I am depressed and other times I am the opposite: I will have lots of ideas and seem like I am moving and thinking really fast. I may also talk very fast. You may or may not have seen me when I have symptoms, and much of the time I am fine."

7. Be ready to answer questions about your illness and what it means for those around you, including colleagues and managers if you are telling your employer. Give the other person a list of resources, including books—such as this one and *Bipolar 101*, which spends a lot more time explaining the illness and its symptoms—and websites about bipolar disorder. Bringing a brochure to the conversation is a very helpful gesture, because it can provide answers to questions the person may not want to ask you directly, or only think of after your conversation is overa. There are several free brochures available online, including from the National Institute of Mental Health, the National Alliance on Mental Illness, and the Depression and Bipolar Support Alliance. In the resources section you will find the exact URLs of these brochures. The latter two organizations also provide lots of resources for loved ones on their websites.

8. If there is something in particular that this person can do to support your wellness program, you may choose to introduce this topic after all questions have been answered and you feel that the person is supportive. Or you may choose to bring this up in a follow-up conversation, to give the person more time to digest what you have said.

What to Do with a Negative Response

If you are met with rejection, anger, sadness, fear, or any sort of misunderstanding when you tell someone about your bipolar disorder, here are a few ways to respond:

- "I understand that this is a difficult thing to hear, and I will give you the time you need to become more used to the idea. I will answer any ongoing questions you may have, but here is a brochure that may help you better understand what I have just shared."

- "I am sorry you feel that way. If you ever want to talk more about it, I am willing to have this conversation again and answer whatever questions you may have. Here is a brochure that may answer more of your questions."

- "I was not expecting this response from you, and although my feelings are hurt, I know that this is a difficult thing to hear about someone you love; if you are afraid about what my bipolar disorder means, I can give you some resources that may answer whatever questions you may have."

Rejection hurts, especially from someone close to you. For this reason, when appropriate you may want to enlist help in disclosing your disorder to people in your life. For example, after talking with your romantic partner, you can ask him or her to join you in speaking with family members and mutual friends. Telling others as a team may provide you with the emotional support you need. As discussed, you may also engage your psychotherapist to help you by inviting your romantic partner, family members, or friends to join you in a therapy session.

Decide Whom You Want to Tell

Make a list of the people you plan to tell about your bipolar disorder, in order of importance, with the most important person first. When making this list, consider how supportive each person will likely be, how close your relationship is, and what his or her experience with your bipolar disorder has been. For example, if someone has had to deal directly with your manic or depressive symptoms, then being able to explain your behavior will be helpful to him or her and to your relationship. If you cannot have a face-to-face conversation, you may choose to tell people by phone, by e-mail, or in a letter, depending on the circumstances and what makes you feel most comfortable.

POTENTIAL MEMBERS OF YOUR SOCIAL SUPPORT NETWORK

Name	Relationship	Phone	E-mail	Address

List as many people as are relevant to your life. If you cannot list at least three people, then it is time to work on building a support network of friends, family, or colleagues whom you can call when you need support in preventing bipolar relapse. (A downloadable version of the above card can be found at http://www.newharbinger.com/28814.)

ADDING PEOPLE TO YOUR SUPPORT NETWORK

If you do not have much of a social support network, you will need to connect with people who can help you stay well. In other words, it is time for you to start making friends. Keep in mind that a social support network increases your feeling of connection to the world around you and allows you to help others as well as receive help yourself. Making friends will not only give you people to lean on, but also make you feel good and decrease your likelihood of feeling depressed.

Friends usually share an interest in a particular activity or topic. Seek out people who are passionate about the same things you are or with whom you have something in common. Join a book club, knitting group, or chess club, if you might enjoy it. Other great ways to meet like-minded people with whom you can develop mutually supportive friendships are to join a support group, take classes at a community college, spend more time with your coworkers, enroll in a group exercise program, and attend church or other religious services.

Connecting with People in a Support Group

To find a support group in your area, visit the website of the National Alliance on Mental Illness (NAMI, http://www.nami.org) or the Depression and Bipolar Support Alliance (DBSA, http://www.dbsalliance.org) or contact their offices, or inquire with your mental health care provider. Or you may want to try an online support group. Online support groups allow you to get support whenever you need it, from a large group of people around the country or even around the world.

The support group that you choose should be one with whose philosophy you agree. For example, some groups tend to be anti-pharmaceuticals and more focused on alternative treatments; others may focus on a lifestyle approach to treatment. If the group meets in person, the time and location of meetings are another important consideration. And, if there is a group facilitator, check to see what his or her qualifications are and what experience he or she has with running such a group. He or she should have a degree in social work, counseling, psychology, nursing, or medicine, as well experience in running these kinds of groups. For self-run groups, you should feel comfortable with the process of the group and the way leadership is structured. You will know that a support group is right for you if you feel comfortable and safe sharing your feelings and thoughts with the group and sense that you are supported by the people in the group. You may find the right group for you on the first try, or you may have to visit several until you find a support group that feels like "home."

Connecting with Classmates

If you are taking a class, perhaps you spend a lot of time in class working in small groups. To begin a friendship, try approaching one of your fellow group members or someone with whom you have already had a casual conversation before, during, or after class. Say hello and talk about something that happened in class. Then invite the other person to have coffee, see a movie, grab a bite, or shop for books or other supplies related to your class. You may not make a connection on your first attempt, but the effort it takes to keep trying will be worth the payoff in social support.

Connecting with Coworkers

If you have colleagues with whom you have developed a good working relationship, you may want to invite them to a social event like bowling or a movie outside of working hours. You can also make an effort to go along with your coworkers when they go out in groups. Making an effort to incorporate yourself into the group will make you more likely to develop friends at work. Even if they are only friends in the work environment, they are people you can trust to help you when work becomes challenging.

Connecting with People in Other Types of Groups

If you attend a group exercise program—for example, a yoga or spinning class—you may have developed a friendly relationship with someone who shares your commitment to staying healthy through exercise. Perhaps there is someone you regularly talk to before, during, or after your exercise program. You may want to invite this person to coffee or a smoothie after your exercise class and see how your friendship grows from there.

Some people find comfort in having spiritual support. If this resonates with you, then faith-based institutions are also a good place to find people with whom to cultivate friendships. Most faith-based institutions offer opportunities for social networking. Spiritual support may also include various affinity groups, many of which provide opportunities for volunteering. Because it feels good to help others, volunteering is one way to prevent or alleviate symptoms of depression.

SEVEN STEPS TO ASKING FOR HELP

In our individualistic culture that emphasizes independence, it can be difficult to admit to yourself that you need help and harder still to ask for the help you need. Asking for help takes courage, but it is evidence of your commitment to maintaining your mental health. Your pride is not worth your health. In addition, asking for help allows other people to feel good as a result of providing support. Most people expect that their friends will request help from time to time. People who really care about you want to see you healthy and will be ready to give you the help you need, if you are ready to ask for it.

1. Choose whom to ask for help by considering each person's ability to provide what you need. If you need someone to drive you around on errands, who is familiar enough with your town? If you need someone to take care of your pets or plants, who is attentive enough for the job? If you need someone to drive you to and from doctor's appointments, whose schedule would permit this? If you need help with your children, who already has a good relationship with them and has the time and energy to take care of them? Also consider how much help someone has provided in the past. If someone has given you a great deal of help, that person may need a break. If someone has never seemed interested in providing help to you, you may still want to ask, but do not be surprised if he or she declines. You may also want to look for more than one person to help you with whatever it is you need help with.

2. Just as when you are telling people about your bipolar disorder, when you need to ask for help, do it in a quiet place at a time when you are not likely to be distracted.

3. Explain your position using statements beginning with "I need" or "I feel." Follow up with "It would be helpful if you could…" or "I could use help [doing…]." If you have already

explained your bipolar symptoms and how they affect you, you could also say, "I am feeling very/a little depressed/manic and it would be helpful if…."

4. Be specific about what you need. For example, if you need help with your children, tell the person what kind of help you need with them, when you need that help, and for how long.

5. Give the person the opportunity to ask questions that will help him or her get a clear understanding of what you need and how best he or she may be able to help.

6. If the person is willing to help, thank him or her for the offer.

   If not, thank him or her for giving it some consideration. Do not feel that someone's inability to help is a reflection of a weak friendship. It may simply be that he or she cannot help you in the way that you need at this time. Reach out for emotional support from others, including your health care providers, to help you deal with any negative feelings about your request for assistance being rejected. Ask your mental health care provider to help you problem solve in advance of your next request for support.

7. After you get the help you need, remember to thank the person or people who helped you.

YOUR CRISIS PLAN

You may follow all the advice given in this book, take your medications as prescribed, and regularly visit your therapist and still find yourself having a mood episode. Because you may find it hard to take care of yourself at such times, it is helpful to plan ahead. Planning for a mental health crisis will help you get the treatment you need quickly and effectively. Including members of your social support network in your crisis plan and sharing it with them will allow them to act on your behalf if you are experiencing symptoms and are in denial about needing help or are unable to ask for it yourself.

Your crisis plan should include the following:

- A list of everyone in your social support network, including their role in your life and their contact information

- A list of all medications you are taking and why you are taking them

- Contact information for your health care providers and your pharmacy

- A list of symptoms that may indicate a need for you to have others take over your care

- A list of instructions for members of your social support network should you not be able to take care of yourself

  This should include information for practical things like paying your bills and making financial decisions. Your partner may be best suited for this role, especially if you have joint accounts.

- A list of people who are available to drive you to appointments or to the hospital, if this becomes necessary

- Directions for care of your children and pets in case you are unable to take care of them

- Directions for notifying your employer and loved ones in the case of hospitalization

- Your health insurance information

- If you choose, an advance medical directive and a legal power of attorney that will be implemented if you are unable to care for yourself

  These should be prepared in consultation with your doctor and legal counsel, respectively.

All this information is best kept in a folder in a central location known to more than one member of your support system. Your health care provider should also have a copy of this information. You may also choose to provide copies to one or two people whom you have a close relationship with and can trust to implement your requests. Lastly, to enable others to get you some help fast, you may want to keep in your wallet an emergency card (or piece of paper) that has your health insurance number, at least three emergency contacts, and the names and phone numbers of your health care providers.

YOUR SOCIAL SUPPORT NETWORK DIRECTORY

It may be a good idea to list all the members of your social support network in one place. This will give you something that makes it easy to see who you can turn to for help in various situations.

To get started, talk with the members of your support network and discuss what kind of support they are willing to give should you need it. Review the chapter for ideas, and mention these common forms of support: emotional support, financial support, child care support, household support, appointment support, and crisis support. Your goal in doing this is to prevent surprising someone with an emergency request for help when he or she has not previously agreed to help in that area. These conversations will not be easy, but they may not be as hard as you think, either, especially with people who care about you. It is better to do this when you are healthy, when you can make good decisions and are not experiencing bipolar symptoms that may negatively influence your interpersonal relationships.

Then write the names and contact information of one to three people who could provide you with each of the forms of support mentioned. As discussed, your health care providers can help you decide who would be best to help you in each area. If you want, you can specify exactly what kind of support you may need—for example, you might break child care support down into "Take the kids to school," "Pick the kids up from school," and "Watch the kids as needed," and write a different name for each one. You may not be able to come up with three names for each form of support, and some names may be repeated. For example, your spouse or partner may show up in all the categories. However, you should have at least three different people in your support network. You can make it a goal to build up your social support network over time. In the meantime, do not forget that you can seek emotional or crisis support from hotlines, support groups, and your mental health care provider's on-call staff.

YOUR SOCIAL SUPPORT NETWORK DIRECTORY

Type of Support: (Specify)	Name	E-mail	Phone
Emotional:			
Emotional:			
Emotional:			
Material:			

Material:			
Material:			
Financial:			
Financial:			
Financial:			
Treatment:			
Treatment:			
Treatment:			
Group:			

Group:			
Group:			
Crisis:			
Crisis:			
Crisis:			
Other:			

SUMMARY

Making friends can be challenging, and telling your friends and family that you have a mental illness can be challenging. However, having an active social support network that provides you with emotional and material assistance when you need it is key to staving off bipolar relapse and reducing the impact of any mood episodes that you do experience.

Your doctor, therapist, nurse, and other health care providers are an important part of your social support network. In order to bring other people, such as family members and friends, into your support network, you will have to disclose your bipolar disorder to them. This is never easy, but the more time you put into planning your conversations about your bipolar disorder, the more productive those conversations will be, no matter how they turn out.

Identify the people in your support network in a chart so that when you need them you have a system in place for making use of this most valuable resource: the people you care about and who care about you.

Asking for support is difficult, but once you have decided on the best sources for each type of assistance, it will be easier to think about ways of asking for help. Asking for help also means being willing to suffer rejection and disappointment; but the more carefully you think these requests through, the better they will go, the deeper and stronger your friendships will be, and the healthier you will be.

CONCLUSION

This book has given you tools for preventing bipolar relapse. Having a chronic, severe illness such as bipolar disorder can be challenging and often overwhelming. Your goal in learning to manage your symptoms and your risk of mood episodes is to find a lifestyle that minimizes your bipolar symptoms and that allows you to do the things you enjoy with people you care about.

There is never a magic bullet for an illness as complex as bipolar disorder, but with good **sleep**, healthy **nutrition**, physical **activity**, and relationships with supportive **people** (SNAP!), you can live the kind of lifestyle that promotes physical and psychological well-being and helps prevent bipolar relapse. By adhering to your medication regimen and tracking your symptoms, mood, and strategies for success, you can reduce the psychic and physical pain that comes with bipolar disorder—not just for yourself, but also for those around you. Building a routine out of healthy habits and monitoring your behavior and symptoms will support a stable lifestyle that will help reduce your likelihood of having a relapse.

RESOURCES

ORGANIZATIONS

Depression and Bipolar Support Alliance
    730 N. Franklin St., Ste. 501
    Chicago, IL 60654-7225
    Toll-free: 800-826-3632
    · Fax: 312-642-7243
    http://www.dbsalliance.org

National Alliance on Mental Illness
    3803 N. Fairfax Dr., Ste. 100
    Arlington, VA 22203-9699
    Phone: 703-524-7600
    Toll-free helpline: 800-950-6264
    Fax: 703-524-9094
    http://www.nami.org
    (Check your local listings for a branch near you.)

National Institute of Mental Health
    National Institutes of Health
    Science Writing, Press, and Dissemination Branch
    6001 Executive Blvd., Rm. 6200, MSC 9663
    Bethesda, MD 20892-9663

Phone: 301-443-4513
Toll-free: 866-615-6464
nimhinfo@nih.gov
http://www.nimh.nih.gov

International Bipolar Foundation
8895 Towne Centre Dr., Ste. 105-360
San Diego, CA 92122-5542
Phone: 858-764-2496
Fax: 858-764-2491
http://www.internationalbipolarfoundation.org

Mental Health America
2000 N. Beauregard St., 6th Floor
Alexandria, VA 22311-1749
Toll-free: 800-969-6642
http://www.mentalhealthamerica.net

National Hopeline Network
Toll-free: 800-784-2433
http://www.hopeline.com

READING LIST

ONLINE BROCHURES

Bipolar Disorder
http://www.nimh.nih.gov/health/publications/bipolar-disorder
-easy-to-read/index.shtml

Bipolar Disorder
http://www.nami.org/Content/NavigationMenu/Mental
_Illnesses/Bipolar1/bipolardisorderbrochure-lores.pdf

Educational Articles
http://www.ibpf.org/articles/educational-articles

Various publications
http://www.dbsalliance.org/site/
PageServer?pagename=education_brochures_print

BOOKS

The Bipolar Disorder Answer Book: Answers to More Than 275 of Your Most Pressing Questions. By Charles Atkins. Naperville, IL: Sourcebooks, 2007.

The Bipolar Workbook: Tools for Controlling Your Mood Swings. By Monica Ramirez Basco. New York: Guilford Press, 2006.

Bipolar Disorder: A Guide for the Newly Diagnosed. By Janelle M. Caponigro, Erica H. Lee, Sheri L. Johnson, and Ann M. Kring. Oakland, CA: New Harbinger Publications, 2012.

Bipolar Happens! 35 Tips to Manage Bipolar Disorder Successfully. By Julie A. Fast. Grayson OmniMedia, Kindle edition.

Take Charge of Bipolar Disorder: A 4-Step Plan for You and Your Loved Ones to Manage the Illness and Create Lasting Stability. By Julie A. Fast and John Preston. New York: Warner Wellness, 2006.

Facing Bipolar: The Young Adult's Guide to Dealing with Bipolar Disorder. By Russ Federman and J. Anderson Thomson. Oakland, CA: New Harbinger Publications, 2010.

Madness: A Bipolar Life. By Marya Hornbacher. Boston: Houghton Mifflin, 2008.

Healthy Living with Bipolar Disorder. A publication of the International Bipolar Foundation. San Diego, CA 2012.

An Unquiet Mind: A Memoir of Moods and Madness. By Kay Redfield Jamison. New York: A. A. Knopf, 1995.

Touched with Fire: Manic-Depressive Illness and the Artistic Temperament. By Kay Redfield Jamison. New York: Free Press, 1993.

The Natural Medicine Guide to Bipolar Disorder, new revised edition. By Stephanie Marohn. Charlottesville, VA: Hampton Roads, 2011.

My Bipolar World: A Collection of Works. By Sylvia Meier. CreateSpace Independent Publishing, 2013.

The Bipolar Disorder Survival Guide: What You and Your Family Need to Know, 2nd edition. By David J. Miklowitz. New York: Guilford Press, 2011.

The Bipolar Teen: What You Can Do to Help Your Child and Your Family. By David J. Miklowitz and Elizabeth L. George. New York: Guilford Press, 2008.

Bipolar 101: A Practical Guide to Identifying Triggers, Managing Medications, Coping with Symptoms, and More. By Ruth C. White and John D. Preston. Oakland, CA: New Harbinger Publications, 2009.

Practical Management of Bipolar Disorder. Edited by Allan H. Young, I. Nicol Ferrier, and Erin E. Michalak. Cambridge: Cambridge University Press, 2010.

REFERENCES

Ali, I. I., L. Schuh, G. L. Barkley, and J. R. Gates. 2004. "Antiepileptic Drugs and Reduced Bone Mineral Density." *Epilepsy and Behavior* 5: 296–300.

Alsuwaidan, M. T., A. Kucyi, C. W. Y. Law, and R. S. McIntyre. 2009. "Exercise and Bipolar Disorder: A Review of Neurobiological Mediators." *Neuromolecular Medicine* 11: 328–36.

Altman, S., S. Haeri, L. J. Cohen, A. Ten, E. Barron, I. I. Galynker, and K. N. Duhamel. 2006. "Predictors of Relapse in Bipolar Disorder: A Review." *Journal of Psychiatric Practice* 12: 269–82.

American Academy of Sleep Medicine. 2012a. "Insomnia: Overview and Facts." http://sleepeducation.com/sleep-disorders/insomnia /overview-facts

———. 2012b. "Insomnia: Symptoms and Causes." http://sleepeduca tion.com/sleep-disorders/insomnia/symptoms-causes

American Psychiatric Association (APA). 2013. *Diagnostic and Statistical Manual of Mental Disorders*. 5th edition, Arlington, VA: American Psychiatric Publishing.

Baglioni, C., G. Battagliese, B. S. Feige, K. Spiegelhalder, C. Nissen, U. Voderholzer, C. Lombardo, and D. Riemann. 2011. "Insomnia as a Predictor of Depression: A Meta-analytical Evaluation of

Longitudinal Epidemiological Studies." *Journal of Affective Disorders* 135: 10–19.

Barone, J. J., and H. R. Roberts. 1996. "Caffeine Consumption." *Food and Chemical Toxicology* 34: 119–29.

Childs, E., and H. de Wit. 2006. "Subjective, Behavioral, and Physiological Effects of Acute Caffeine in Light, Nondependent Caffeine Users." *Psychopharmacology* 185: 514–23.

Chiu, C. C., S. Y. Huang, C. C. Chen, and K. P. Su. 2005. "Omega-3 Fatty Acids Are More Beneficial in the Depressive Phase Than in the Manic Phase in Patients with Bipolar I Disorder." Letter to the editor. *Journal of Clinical Psychiatry* 66: 1613–14.

Clayton, E. H., T. L. Janstock, S. J. Hirneth, C. J. Kable, M. L. Garg, and P. L. Hazell. 2009. "Reduced Mania and Depression in Juvenile Bipolar Disorder Associated with Long-Chain Omega-3 Polyunsaturated Fatty Acid Supplementation." *European Journal of Clinical Nutrition* 63: 1037–40.

Davidson, K. M., and B. J. Kaplan. 2012. "Nutrient Intakes Are Correlated with Overall Psychiatric Functioning in Adults with Mood Disorders." *Canadian Journal of Psychiatry* 57: 85–92.

Eidelman, P., A. Gershon, K. Kaplan, E. McGlinchey, and A. G. Harvey. 2012. "Social Support and Social Strain in Inter-episode Bipolar Disorder." *Bipolar Disorders* 14: 628–40.

Eriksson, S., and G. Gard. 2011. "Physical Exercise and Depression." *Physical Therapy Reviews* 16: 261–68.

Ewing, J. A. 1984. "Detecting Alcoholism: The CAGE Questionnaire." *Journal of the American Medical Association* 252: 1905–7.

Frank, E., J. M. Gonzalez, and A. Fagiolini. 2006. "The Importance of Routine for Preventing Recurrence in Bipolar Disorder." *American Journal of Psychiatry* 163: 981–85.

Freeman, M. P., J. R. Hibbeln, K. L. Wisner, J. M. Davis, D. Mischoulon, M. Peet, et al. 2006. "Omega-3 Fatty Acids: Evidence Basis for Treatment and Future Research in Psychiatry." *Journal of Clinical Psychiatry* 67: 1954–67.

Gamaldo, C. E., A. K. Shaikh, and J. C. McArthur. 2012. "The Sleep-Immunity Relationship." *Neurologic Clinics* 30: 1313–43.

Goldstein, B. I., V.P. Velyvis, and S. V. Parikh. 2006. "The Association Between Moderate Alcohol Use and Illness Severity in Bipolar Disorder: A Preliminary Report." *Journal of Clinical Psychiatry* 67: 102–6.

Gonzalez-Bono, E., N. Rohleder, D. H. Hellhammer, A. Salvador, and C. Kirschbaum. 2002. "Glucose but Not Protein or Fat Load Amplifies the Cortisol Response to Psychosocial Stress." *Hormones and Behavior* 41: 328–33.

Grover, K. W., R. D. Goodwin, and M. J. Zvolensky. 2012. "Does Current Versus Former Smoking Play a Role in the Relationship Between Anxiety and Mood Disorders and Nicotine Dependence?" *Addictive Behaviors* 37: 682–85.

Gruber, J. M., D. J. Miklowitz, A. G. Harvey, E. Frank, D. Kupfer, M. E. Thase, G. S. Sachs, and T. A. Ketter. 2011. "Sleep Matters: Sleep Functioning and Course of Illness in Bipolar Disorder." *Journal of Affective Disorders* 134: 416–20.

Hall-Flavin, D. K. 2012. *Bipolar Medications and Weight Gain,* accessed May 25, 2013, from http://www.mayoclinic.com/health/bipolar-medications-and-weight-gain/AN02062

Harvard Medical School. 2013. "Defining 'Moderate Intensity Exercise.'" *Focus on Fitness* (e-mail newsletter, March 11, 2013).

Hong, J., C. Reed, D. Novick, J. M. Haro, and J. Aguado. 2011. "Clinical and Economic Consequences of Medication Non-adherence in the Treatment of Patients with a Manic/Mixed Episode of Bipolar Disorder: Results from the European Mania in

Bipolar Longitudinal Evaluation of Medication (EMBLEM) study." *Psychiatry Research* 190: 110–14.

Jónsdóttir, H., S. Opjordsmoen, A. B. Birkenaes, C. Simonsen, J. A. Engh, P. A. Ringen, A. Vaskinn, S. Friis, K. Sundet, and O. A. Andreassen. 2013. "Predictors of Medication Adherence in Patients with Schizophrenia and Bipolar Disorder." *Acta Psychiatrica Scandinavica* 127: 23–33.

Júdice, P. B., J. P. Magalhães, D. A. Santos, C. N. Matias, A. I. Carita, P. A. S. Armada-Da-Silva, L. B. Sardinha, and A. M. Silva. 2013. "A Moderate Dose of Caffeine Ingestion Does Not Change Energy Expenditure but Decreases Sleep Time in Physically Active Males: A Double-Blind Randomized Controlled Trial." *Journal of Applied Physiology, Nutrition, and Metabolism* 38: 49–56.

Keck, P. E., and S. L. McElroy. 2006. "Bipolar Disorder, Obesity, and Pharmacotherapy-Associated Weight Gain." *Journal of Clinical Psychiatry* 64: 1426–35.

Kerkhofs, M., and K. Z. Boudjeltia. 2012. "From Total Sleep Deprivation to Cardiovascular Disease: A Key Role for the Immune System?" *Sleep: Journal of Sleep and Sleep Disorders Research,* 35: 885–96.

Khamba, B., M. Aucoin, D. Tsirgielis, A. Copeland, M. Vermani, C. Cameron, I. Szpindel, B. Laidlaw, I. Epstein, and M. Katzman. 2011. "Effectiveness of Vitamin D in the Treatment of Mood Disorders: A Literature Review." *Journal of Orthomolecular Medicine* 26: 127–35.

Kilbourne, A. M., D. L. Rofey, J. F. McCarthy, E. P. Post, D. Welsh, and F. C. Blow. 2007. "Nutrition and Exercise Behavior Among Patients with Bipolar Disorder." *Bipolar Disorders* 9: 443–52.

Layman, D. K. 2009. "*Dietary Guidelines* Should Reflect New Understandings About Adult Protein Needs." Commentary. *Nutrition and Metabolism* 6: 12.

Lilja, J. J., K. Laitinen, and P. J. Neuvonen. 2005. "Effects of Grapefruit Juice on the Absorption of Levothyroxine." *British Journal of Clinical Pharmacology* 60: 337–41.

Liperoti, R., F. Landi, O. Fusco, R. Bernabei, and G. Onder. 2009. "Omega-3 Polyunsaturated Fatty Acids and Depression: A Review of the Evidence." *Current Pharmaceutical Design* 15: 4165–72.

Mayo Clinic. 2011. "Exercise: 7 Benefits of Regular Physical Activity." http://www.mayoclinic.com/health/exercise/HQ01676

———. 2013. "Healthy Diet: Do You Follow Dietary Guidelines?" http://www.mayoclinic.com/health/how-to-eat-healthy/MY 02264

McGrath, C. L., S. J. Glatt, P. Sklar, H. Le-Niculescu, R. Kuczenski, A. E. Doyle, et al. 2009. "Evidence for Genetic Association of RORB with Bipolar Disorder." *BMC Psychiatry* 9: 70.

National Consumers League. 2011. "US Surgeon General Joins with NCL to Launch Medication Adherence Awareness Campaign, Script Your Future." http://www.nclnet.org/newsroom/press -releases/503-us-surgeon-general-joins-with-ncl-to-launch -medication-adherence-awareness-campaign-script-your-future

National Health Service (UK). 2013. "What Is Moderate and Vigorous Exercise?" http://www.nhs.uk/chq/Pages/2419.aspx?CategoryID =52&#0022;SubCategoryID=145

National Sleep Foundation. 2013. "How Much Sleep Do We Really Need?" http://www.sleepfoundation.org/article/how-sleep-works /how-much-sleep-do-we-really-need

Neumeister, A. 2003. "National Institute for Mental Health's Mood and Anxiety Disorder's Program." *Psychopharmacology Bulletin* 37: 99–115.

National Heart, Lung, and Blood Institute (NHLBI). 2003. *National Sleep Disorders Research Plan, 2003*. Bethesda, MD: National Institutes of Health.

NHS Choices. 2012. "10 Tips to Beat Insomnia." http://www.nhs.uk /Livewell/insomnia/Pages/insomniatips.aspx

National Institute of General Medical Sciences (NIGMS). 2013. *Circadian Rhythms Fact Sheet*. http://www.nigms.nih.gov/Edu cation/Pages/Factsheet_CircadianRhythms.aspx

National Institutes of Health (NIH). 2011, December. "Weighing In on Dietary Fats." *News in Health*. http://newsinhealth.nih.gov /issue/dec2011

————. "Recommendations for Physical Activity." http://www.nhlbi .nih.gov/health/health-topics/phys/recommend.html

National Institute of Mental Health (NIMH). N.d. "Bipolar Disorder." http://www.nimh.nih.gov/health/topics/bipolar-disorder/index .shtml

National Institute of Neurological Disorders and Stroke (NINDS). 2007. "Brain Basics: Understanding Sleep." http://www.ninds.nih .gov/disorders/brain_basics/understanding_sleep.htm

Otto, M., and J. A. J. Smits. 2011. *Exercise for Mood and Anxiety: Proven Strategies for Overcoming Depression and Enhancing Well-Being*. New York: Oxford University Press.

Parker, G., N. A. Gibson, H. Brotchie, G. Heruc, A.-M. Rees, and D. Hadzi-Pavlovic. 2006. "Omega-3 Fatty Acids and Mood Disorders." *American Journal of Psychiatry* 163: 969–78.

Parker, G., I. Parker, and H. Brotchie. 2006. "Mood State Effects of Chocolate." *Journal of Affective Disorders* 92: 149–59.

Pate, R. R., M. Pratt, S. N. Blair, W. L. Haskell, C. A. Macera, C. Bouchard, et al. 1995. "Physical Activity and Public Health: A Recommendation from the Centers for Disease Control and

Prevention and the American College of Sports Medicine." *Journal of the American Medical Association* 273: 402–7.

Perlman, C. A., S. L. Johnson, and T. A. Mellman. 2006. "The Prospective Impact of Sleep Duration on Depression and Mania." *Bipolar Disorders* 8: 271–74.

Piri, M., S. Zardoshtian, S. Khazaee, and R. Piri. 2012. "The Effect of Eight Weeks of Aerobic Training on Reducing Mood Disorders, Depression and Mania in High School Students High School Boys." *International Journal of Academic Research in Business and Social Sciences* 2: 267–73.

Poulin, M-J., L. Cortese, R. Williams, N. Wine, and R. S. McIntyre. 2005. "Atypical Antipsychotics in Psychiatric Practice: Practical Implications for Clinical Monitoring." *The Canadian Journal of Psychiatry / La Revue Canadienne de Psychiatrie* 50: 555–62.

Pratchett, L. 2010. "Social Support in Bipolar Disorder: The Relationship Between Social Support and Mood Symptoms." PsyD dissertation, Palo Alto University. ProQuest (AAT 3396776).

Ratanawongsa, N., A. J. Karter, M. M. Parker, C. R. Lyles, M. Heisler, H. H. Moffet, N. Adler, E. M. Warton, and D. Schillinger. 2013. "Communication and Medication Refill Adherence: The Diabetes Study of Northern California." *JAMA Internal Medicine* 173: 210–18.

Rogers, P. J., K. M. Appleton, D. Kessler, T. J. Peters, D. Gunnell, R. C. Hayward, S. V. Heatherley, L. M. Christian, S. A. McNaughton, and A. R. Ness. 2008. "No Effect of n-3 Long-Chain Polyunsaturated Fatty Acid (EPA and DHA) Supplementation on Depressed Mood and Cognitive Function: A Randomised Controlled Trial." *British Journal of Nutrition* 99: 421–31.

Saito, M., M. Hirata-Koizumi, M. Matsumoto, T. Urano, and R. Hasegawa. 2005. "Undesirable Effects of Citrus Juice on the

Pharmacokinetics of Drugs: Focus on Recent Studies." *Drug Safety* 8: 677–94.

Sajatovic, M., M. Valenstein, F. C. Blow, D. Ganoczy, and R. V. Ignacio. 2006. "Treatment Adherence with Antipsychotic Medications in Bipolar Disorder." *Bipolar Disorders* 8: 232–41.

Sarris, J., D. Mischoulon, and I. Schweitzer. 2011. "Adjunctive Nutraceuticals with Standard Pharmacotherapies in Bipolar Disorder: A Systematic Review of Clinical Trials." *Bipolar Disorders* 13: 454–65.

Seden, K., L. Dickinson, S. Khoo, and D. Back. 2010. "Grapefruit-Drug Interactions." *Drugs* 70: 2373–407.

Shabbir, F., A. Patel, C. Mattison, S. Bose, R. Krishnamohan, E. Sweeney, et al. 2013. "Effect of Diet on Serotonergic Neuro-transmission in Depression." *Neurochemistry International* 62: 324–29.

Silverstone, P. H., and T. Silverstone. 2004. "A Review of Acute Treatments for Bipolar Depression." *International Clinical Psycho-pharmacology* 19: 113–24.

Spaeth, A. M., D. F. Dinges, and N. Goel. 2013. "Effects of Experimental Sleep Restriction on Weight Gain, Caloric Intake, and Meal Timing in Healthy Adults." *Journal of Sleep and Sleep Disorders Research* 36: 981–90.

Srinivasan, V., M. Smits, W. Spence, A. D. Lowe, L. Kayumov, S. R. Pandi-Perumal, B. Parry, and D. P. Cardinali. 2006. "Melatonin in Mood Disorders." *World Journal of Biological Psychiatry* 7: 138–51.

Stahl, L. A., D. P. Begg, R. S. Weisinger, and A. J. Sinclair. 2008. "The Role of Omega-3 Fatty Acids in Mood Disorders." *Current Opinion in Investigational Drugs* 9: 57–64.

Stevens, C. J., and A. D. Bryan. 2012. "Rebranding Exercise: There's an App for That." *American Journal of Health Promotion* 27: 69–70.

Sullivan, A. E., C. M. Judd, D. A. Axelson, and D. J. Miklowitz. 2012. "Family Functioning and the Course of Adolescent Bipolar Disorder." *Behavior Therapy* 43: 837–47.

Tudor-Locke, C., and Bassett, D. R., Jr. 2004. "How Many Steps/Day Are Enough? Preliminary Pedometer Indices for Public Health." *Sports Medicine* 34:1–8.

US Department of Agriculture Center for Nutrition Policy and Promotion. 2011. "10 Tips to a Great Plate." http://www.choosemy plate.gov/food-groups/downloads/TenTips/DGTipsheet 1ChooseMyPlate-BlkAndWht.pdf

US Department of Health and Human Services. 1996. *Physical Activity and Health: A Report of the Surgeon General.* Atlanta: Author. http://www.cdc.gov/nccdphp/sgr/pdf/sgrfull.pdf

WHO (World Health Organization). 2003. "Adherence to Long-Term Therapies: Evidence for Action." http://apps.who.int/iris/bitstream /10665/42682/1/9241545992.pdf

Wildes, J. E., M. D. Marcus, and A. Fagiolini. 2006. "Obesity in Patients with Bipolar Disorder: A Biopsychosocial-Behavioral Model." *Journal of Clinical Psychiatry* 67: 904–15.

Williams, D. J., and W. B. Strean. 2006. "Physical Activity Promotion in Social Work." *Social Work* 51: 180–84.

Ruth C. White, PhD, MPH, MSW, is clinical associate professor at the University of Southern California's School of Social Work and has taught undergraduate and graduate students in social work for fifteen years. White received her MSW from McGill University and her PhD and MPH from the University of California, Berkeley. She has worked as a social worker in Canada, the US, and the UK in various types of social work settings, and she keeps a blog at bipolar-101.blogspot.com. To find out more about White, visit ruthcwhite.com.

FROM OUR PUBLISHER—

As the publisher at New Harbinger and a clinical psychologist since 1978, I know that emotional problems are best helped with evidence-based therapies. These are the treatments derived from scientific research (randomized controlled trials) that show what works. Whether these treatments are delivered by trained clinicians or found in a self-help book, they are designed to provide you with proven strategies to overcome your problem.

Therapies that aren't evidence-based—whether offered by clinicians or in books—are much less likely to help. In fact, therapies that aren't guided by science may not help you at all. That's why this New Harbinger book is based on scientific evidence that the treatment can relieve emotional pain.

This is important: if this book isn't enough, and you need the help of a skilled therapist, use the following resources to find a clinician trained in the evidence-based protocols appropriate for your problem. And if you need more support—a community that understands what you're going through and can show you ways to cope—resources for that are provided below, as well.

Real help is available for the problems you have been struggling with. The skills you can learn from evidence-based therapies will change your life.

Matthew McKay, PhD
Publisher, New Harbinger Publications

**If you need a therapist, the following organization
can help you find a therapist trained in cognitive behavioral therapy (CBT).**
The Association for Behavioral & Cognitive Therapies (ABCT) Find-a-Therapist service offers a list of therapists schooled in CBT techniques. Therapists listed are licensed professionals who have met the membership requirements of ABCT and who have chosen to appear in the directory.
Please visit www.abct.org and click on *Find a Therapist*.

For additional support for patients, family, and friends, please contact the following:

Anxiety and Depression Association of American (ADAA) **Please visit www.adaa.org**

Depression and Bipolar Support Alliance (DBSA) **Visit www.dbsalliance.org**

National Alliance on Mental Illness (NAMI) **Please visit www.nami.org**

National Suicide Prevention Lifeline **Call 24 hours a day 1-800-273-TALK (8255)
or visit suicidepreventionlifeline.org**

MORE BOOKS *from*
NEW HARBINGER PUBLICATIONS

LOVING SOMEONE WITH BIPOLAR DISORDER, SECOND EDITION

Understanding & Helping
Your Partner

ISBN: 978-1608822195 / US $16.95
Also available as an e-book

THE DIALECTICAL BEHAVIOR THERAPY SKILLS WORKBOOK FOR BIPOLAR DISORDER

Using DBT to Regain Control of
Your Emotions & Your Life

ISBN: 978-1572246287 / US $21.95
Also available as an e-book

WHEN DEPRESSION HURTS YOUR RELATIONSHIP

How to Regain Intimacy &
Reconnect with Your Partner
When You're Depressed

ISBN: 978-1608828326 / US $16.95
Also available as an e-book

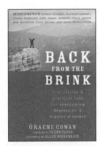

BACK FROM THE BRINK

True Stories & Practical Help for
Overcoming Depression
& Bipolar Disorder

ISBN: 978-1608828562 / US $16.95
Also available as an e-book

THE BIPOLAR II DISORDER WORKBOOK

Managing Recurring Depression,
Hypomania & Anxiety

ISBN: 978-1608827664 / US $21.95
Also available as an e-book

DON'T LET YOUR EMOTIONS RUN YOUR LIFE

How Dialectical Behavior
Therapy Can Put You in Control

ISBN: 978-1572243095 / US $19.95
Also available as an e-book

newharbingerpublications
1-800-748-6273 / newharbinger.com

(VISA, MC, AMEX / prices subject to change without notice)

f Like us on Facebook   t Follow us on Twitter @newharbinger.com

Don't miss out on new books in the subjects that interest you.
Sign up for our **Book Alerts** at **newharbinger.com/bookalerts**

Register your **new harbinger** titles for additional benefits!

When you register your **new harbinger** title—purchased in any format, from any source—you get access to benefits like the following:

- Downloadable accessories like printable worksheets and extra content

- Instructional videos and audio files

- Information about updates, corrections, and new editions

Not every title has accessories, but we're adding new material all the time.

Access free accessories in 3 easy steps:

1. Sign in at NewHarbinger.com (or **register** to create an account).

2. Click on **register a book**. Search for your title and click the **register** button when it appears.

3. Click on the **book cover or title** to go to its details page. Click on **accessories** to view and access files.

That's all there is to it!

If you need help, visit:

NewHarbinger.com/accessories

new harbinger
CELEBRATING
40 YEARS

31901055596771